PRAISE FOR DAN LOK

"Thought-provoking! Entertaining! Mind blowing! His 'Tony Robbins meets Dr. Phil' style is bold, brash, but right on target if you want to know what it really takes to retire young and retire rich. Dan, you are the man!"

- Shane Goldberg, CEO of PhotoshopZoo.com

"Dan Lok is, without a doubt, one of the most ingenious and innovative marketers I've ever come across... and one of the few people whose advice I trust. Listen to what he has to say... THIS guy will help you make a Quantum Leap in your business."

- Daniel S. Peña, Sr., Founder and Chairman of The Guthrie Group
Mr. Peña turned $820 into a $400 million market-valued energy company in just 8 years!

"Dan Lok has an extraordinary way of capturing people's attention through the written word. Dan knows writing and he knows marketing. Most importantly, he is a man who can do exactly what he says he can do, do it exactly when he says he will - and do it with absolute integrity and honesty. If you want to Make It BIG in business, Dan Lok is your man. He has my highest recommendation."

- Frank McKinney, 5-Time International Best Seller
The World's Premier Creator of Oceanfront Multi-Million Dollar Estate Homes

"Dan Lok tells you critical marketing facts that would take years to learn in the real world. He pulls no punches as he shows you clearly how to seriously increase your profits while sidestepping the many mistakes made by ordinary marketers."

- Jay Conrad Levinson, The Father of Guerrilla Marketing
Author of the "Guerrilla Marketing" book series.

"The whole idea of F.U. Money will be a powerful paradigm shift for most people. Dan is blunt, outspoken and brutally honest. You'll learn more practical ideas on how to make more, work less and enjoy life in this book than in any other single source. This book is a must-read."

- Dave Debeau, President of Results Enterprises Inc.
Publisher of "Fast Track Inner Circle" & "B.C. Profit$"

F.U. MONEY

F.U. MONEY

Make As Much Money
As You Damn Well Want
And Live Your Life
As You Damn Well Please!

DAN THE MAN LOK

Published by Elevate, Charleston, South Carolina.
Member of Advantage Media Group.

ELEVATE is a registered trademark and the Elevate colophon is a trademark of Advantage Media Group, Inc.

Printed in the United States of America.

ISBN: 978-1-59932-574-3

This publication is designed to provide accurate and authoritative information in regard to the subject matter covered. It is sold with the understanding that the publisher is not engaged in rendering legal, accounting, or other professional services. If legal advice or other expert assistance is required, the services of a competent professional person should be sought.

Most Advantage Media Group titles are available at special quantity discounts for bulk purchases for sales promotions, premiums, fundraising, and educational use. Special versions or book excerpts can also be created to fit specific needs.

For more information, please write: Special Markets, Advantage Media Group, P.O. Box 272, Charleston, SC 29402 or call 1.866.775.1696.

Visit us online at **advantagefamily**.com

Library of Congress Cataloging-in-Publication Data

Lok, Dan.
F.U. money : make as much money as you damn well want and live your life as you damn well please / Dan The Man Lok.
p. cm.
Includes bibliographical references and index.
ISBN 978-1-59932-147-9 (hbk. : alk. paper)
1. Money--Psychological aspects. 2. Wealth--Psychological aspects. 3. Success.
I. Title.
HG222.3.L65 2009
332.024--dc22

2009020815

TABLE OF CONTENTS

Part 4: The F.U. Money Business 181

INTRODUCTION

You have never read a book like mine.

I am going to make some assumptions here. You are holding this book in your hands because you know where you want to be financially, but you're not there yet.

You're sick and tired of your job, you're frustrated with your financial situation, or you don't have enough cash flowing into your business for you to retire and/or make you rich.

One thing I am sure is that you're reading this book because you want MORE...

MORE money... MORE stuff... MORE satisfaction... MORE time... MORE happiness... MORE sex... MORE fun... MORE love... MORE pleasure... MORE of SOMETHING!

...and that's fucking awesome.

Life is all about wanting more and making more. That's the reality of things, and there's not a damn thing wrong with it. So I'm working on the assumption that you want more and you don't feel guilty about it.

If you do feel guilty about it, realize your guilt is part of the problem. It's a big reason that you don't have more. GET OVER IT.

If you go to the business section of bookstores and libraries, the shelves are packed with all kinds of business and success books—endless rows of personal development and self-help books. Most of these books are a complete waste of your time and money.

The first set of books is the touchy-feely, new age, prosperity-type stuff in the self-help section. The thing is, if you were to actually meet and get to know these so-called "prosperity gurus" in person, you would find out they have no money—they're poor. They don't have a pot to piss in or a window to throw it out of.

So how the hell can they teach you about prosperity when they have no prosperity themselves? Oh, you might say, "Dan, they're rich spiritually." Yeah, right. That's nothing but a lame ass excuse for the prosperity gurus to justify their lack of wealth.

To me, true prosperity means being rich in ALL areas of your life. This includes your home, love life, family, health, friends, fun, and yes, money. Lots of money.

The second set of books is the motivational psycho-babble. These looney-toons tell you that if you recite daily affirmations… think positively enough… if you meditate and visualize… lock yourself in a room with purple candles and some hippy-smelling incense… that somehow money will fall into your lap.

These motivational gurus tell you if you feel good about yourself, you'll make money. I say if you make a ton of money, then you'll feel pretty damn good about yourself.

The third set of books is the business books written by authors who have no real world business experience whatsoever. I particularly can't stand these posers.

These are the business school professors and "paper gurus" who pose as business experts yet have never even started a business in their entire miserable lives.

While their theories might sound good, they're of no help at all because the authors have never been in the trenches. They don't know what it's like to miss a payroll. They don't know what it's like to sell their car, mortgage their house, and live on rice and beans to keep their business alive.

Yet here they are doing "research" and feeding you all this non-sensical data and making it all so complicated that in the end you're so confused that you never implement a damn thing.

Then you have the fourth group of books that attempt to walk you through the step-by-step mechanics of starting, growing, and, ultimately, selling a business.

Stuff like raising capital, marketing, selling, management, leadership, those types of books. Some are great, some are not so good, and some are downright dangerous. But NONE of these books will tell you how to prepare your mind and adjust your perspective for making your F.U. Money.

Lastly, you have the financial books—work hard, save money, live below your means, invest in mutual funds, let compound interest work its magic, and then ONE DAY you'll be able to retire in comfort (not even rich) if you're lucky.

Of course, that is if you have the self-discipline to put away the money, not blow everything you make at the end of every month, and get a high return on your investments for a LOOOONG period of time.

I don't know about you, but I think the idea of working your entire life, as hard as you can, usually at a job you hate, so you can retire and enjoy life, is ludicrous.

Why wait until you're old and gray to retire? Why wait until retirement to start enjoying your life? Why not do it now?

By the way, do you know who most of these financial experts and authors work for? The mutual fund companies! Why do you think these mutual fund companies advertise their retirement plans like crazy? Cause they have your best interest at heart, or cause they make an obscene fortune in fees?

I think you already know the answer.

THE ONLY KINDS OF BOOKS THAT ARE WORTH YOUR TIME

There are a group of books written by people who have achieved a high level of success in business, such as the autobiographies of Richard Branson, Steve Jobs, Bill Gates, Warren Buffet, etc. I love those books. You learn from the successes and failures of people who have been there, done that. Those are the books you should read.

WHY THE HELL SHOULD YOU EVEN LISTEN TO ME?

I came to North America years ago with no money, no connections, and not a word of the English language on my lips. In fact, I still speak with a thick accent. I wasn't born with a silver spoon in my mouth. I started from scratch and made lots and lots of mistakes. I've been screwed over by many people.

I've worked for minimum wage in a supermarket as a grocery bagger. I've been up and down multiple times, at one point $150,000 in debt, and, yet, I made it all back. I became a self-made multi-millionaire NOT because I inherited it when my rich uncle died or somebody gave it to me, but because I made it from scratch, with my sweat and tears... through the cutthroat world of business.

I can retire today if I want to. If I want to hop on a plane tomorrow and go spend a month at a resort in the Caribbean, I can do it—and I have done it.

I am free to do what I want, when I want, where I want, with whomever I want for as long as I want without having to worry about money. And, yes, I can say fuck you to anyone I don't like, anywhere, without consequence because I've made my F.U. Money.

WARNING: PLEASE DO NOT READ THIS BOOK IF YOU'RE EASILY OFFENDED BY STRONG IDEAS OR LANGUAGE

In case you didn't notice, the language in this book is not politically correct. This book is definitely not for the easily-offended or the faint of heart.

In other words, I didn't take the time to edit out all the "shits," "fucks," and other offensive terms. I write the way I talk. No bullshit, no fluff, and no sugar coating. And I think the bad language adds a bit of spice to some of these messages and makes them easier to read.

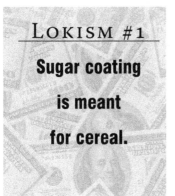

LOKISM #1

Sugar coating is meant for cereal.

I know the title of "F.U. Money" alone will offend a lot of people. However, I believe I'm only as effective to the degree that I am willing to offend. It's better to be hated than ignored. During my business career, I've always had critics and people who don't like me.

So before we dive in, I want to make three things perfectly clear:

1. I didn't invent the ideas or strategies. I simply spell them out in a book. Nothing in this book is original. Anything I've been able to accomplish today has been a direct result of what others have taught me, supported me through, and even challenged me to do.

I think originality is highly overrated. You can always tell the pioneers because they're the ones laying in the sand with arrows in their backs! In fact, most of my fortunes are made by altering existing ideas, not creating something new.

2. You won't find ALL the answers in this book. You'll find some of the answers, but not all of them.

The purpose of this book is NOT to teach you everything there is to know about making your F.U. Money. My goal is to expand your horizons, shift your paradigm, and open your mind to a whole new world of opportunity. As Oliver Wendell Holmes Jr. said, "Man's mind stretched to a new idea never goes back to its original dimensions."

This book is also not a magic pill or silver bullet for the people who are simply wishing and dreaming that money will suddenly "manifest" itself into their lives.

If you believe in that shit, then you shouldn't be reading this book anyway. This book is for serious people who are dedicated to building a business that can give them freedom and prosperity beyond their wildest dreams. But in order to do so, work is involved.

3. I am not asking you to agree with me. In fact, it is perfectly okay to disagree with me—I couldn't care less. There are many ways to be right. What I'm going to share with you are the ways that have proven to be right for me. That doesn't make them right or wrong—it just makes it my experience. And that's the only place I can come from—my experience.

Take my suggestions cafeteria-style if you want. Take one or two ideas and try them out. If they work for you, great—keep them. If they don't work for you, kick them to the curb. No hard feelings whatsoever.

THE SURE-FIRE WAY TO FAILURE

I don't know the sure-fire way to success. But I sure as hell know the sure-fire way to failure, and that is to try to please everybody.

I got rich and happy by not giving a damn what people think. I don't try to please everybody at this point in my life because I've made my F.U. Money.

So FUCK the critics! Those who can't do, criticize. It's easier to sit back and criticize the people who are actually doing something. Here's my message to the critics: "If you're so damn smart, why aren't you rich?"

If you have no critics, you likely have no success. Anyone in the world who is making an impact WILL be criticized—period.

I guarantee that when you start going after your dream and working towards your F.U. Money, you will encounter criticism. So you might as well develop an alligator skin and get used to it.

> "To avoid criticism, do nothing, say nothing, and be nothing."
> – Albert Harris

The key is not to internalize it. Don't take it personally. Critics are losers—so who cares?

Just because you exist in the world, somebody somewhere will be offended. Those people are NOT going to give you money or have anything to do with you anyway. So who gives a shit what they think?

WHAT IS THIS BOOK REALLY ABOUT?

So what is this book really about? This book is about making you a lot of money, about making you believe in yourself like you never have before, about forcing you to take massive action to do whatever the hell it takes to make your F.U. Money.

This is not some touchy-feely, happy-slappy, feel-good book. As you can already see, I am not here for you to like me. If you want a friend, buy a dog.

I am here to show you how to think differently. I am here to change the way you think about business and about making a lot of money. I am here to make you grow. I am here to challenge you. I am here to give you a dose of reality.

There's just no other way. My job is not to make you like me; my job is to get you off your butt to do something.

And I don't care if I have to slap, kick, punch, or drag you to the finish line, that's what I'm prepared to do. I WILL make you feel uncomfortable. I WILL make you feel uneasy. I WILL be in your face.

I am here to tell you what you don't want to hear, but need to hear. You might be put-off by my brutal honesty but you just have to realize that it's "tough love."

One last thing: as you go through this book, ask yourself two questions:

- How does this apply to me?
- How do I take direct action?

To get the maximum value and results from this book, use the "F.U.M.A.—F.U. Money Assignments" throughout different chapters to write down your notes/answers as you go.

Don't just read this book, *use* this book. Grab a pen and a highlighter, feel free to write on it, tear it apart, make a mess of it, whatever you want to do—just as long as you use the damn thing!

Are you ready? Very good. Let's get started...

part 1:
THE F.U.
MONEY
LIFESTYLE

CHAPTER 1

WHAT THE HELL IS F.U. MONEY?

F.U. Money is the "enough is enough" number—when you get to a point when you don't have to take shit from anybody, when you make enough money that you're able to say fuck you to anyone, anywhere (including your boss) without consequence.

F.U. Money means different things for different people. It's a metaphor for freedom—freedom from financial worries that rich people experience... freedom from stress and debt... freedom from a daily office routine. When you have F.U. Money, you have complete, total freedom to live your life the way you want to live it, doing the things you've always wanted to do.

F.U. Money gives you the freedom to choose when and how often you spend quality time with family and friends. It means you can buy things without looking at the price tag. You can contribute money for whatever good cause that's close to your heart. If you want to hand some poor person on the street one hundred dollars, you can do so without any money worries.

When you have F.U. Money, you can buy the vacation home in the mountain or at the beach. You can improve your house and decorate it. You can drive the dream car you've always wanted to own. You can buy the house you've always wanted to live in.

No more sleepless nights worrying about money. When you make your F.U. Money, you never again have to worry about the future of your family. You can provide your kids or grandkids anything they want.

No alarm clock assaulting you in the morning. You can wake up whenever you want and do whatever you want. You can just put "do nothing" on the to-do-list. You can go skiing, golfing, hiking, surfing, biking—whatever you feel like.

F.U. Money means you can travel the world, learn new languages, and meet interesting people. If you want to hop on a plane tomorrow and spend a month at a resort in Hawaii, you can do it. And when you travel, you can fly first class instead of coach.

Or if you're like me, once you've made your F.U. Money, you can dedicate your life to helping other people make their F.U. Money as well. You can mentor others and find ways to make a positive difference. You can choose your work based on what you like to do and what really contributes to other people's lives, not on how much it pays.

F.U. Money allows you to hire a housekeeper and get rid of housework so you can focus your talents where you can be productive and live your passions. You can hire a personal chef if you don't like to cook. You can write the book you've always wanted to write. You can produce the music you've always wanted to produce.

Bottom line is, life is pretty fucking awesome when you have your F.U. Money!

For some people, it might be millions and millions of dollars, but for others it might not be anywhere near that much. However you define it, it's about having so damn much money that you don't need any more... where you could easily and gratefully give it away and still have plenty left over.

It's about living your life on your own terms, according to your possibilities, not your limitations.

Now why is F.U. Money important? Well, put it this way—if you don't make your F.U. Money, you're permanently a slave.

It's not a question of how much money you make. It goes beyond that. F.U. Money is the point of true liberation.

LOKISM #2

F.U. Money is the point of true liberation.

Because if you don't know your F.U. Money amount, you could be making a million dollars a year yet still be stuck in a behavioral pattern as if you have no wealth.

WHEN IS ENOUGH, ENOUGH?

"Money is a mirror. An examination of your money and the way you use money is a way of understanding yourself in the same way that a mirror provides a way of seeing yourself."

- MICHAEL PHILLIPS

At the very beginning of my career, I became obsessed with money, since I made the decision early on that I was going to become rich. I pursued money like nothing else mattered. As a result I sacrificed balance in my family life and fell into a very common trap.

When I first started and didn't have a lot of money, my goal was something like this: "If I could just make fifty thousand dollars a year, wow! That would be awesome!"

And then when I hit fifty thousand dollars I would think to myself and even pray, "You know, just let me double that. If I could make one hundred thousand dollars a year, I wouldn't ask for more..."

And when I got to one hundred thousand dollars I would say to myself, "Well you know, I could get to two hundred thousand... then five hundred thousand... then one million... then two million... then four million." It's never enough. It's interesting to see how quickly we adapt our spending habits to our increased income.

The trap was this: thinking that although what I had was good, it was never quite enough.

That's the danger of pursuing money. The process itself become addictive—and if you're not careful you will get fixated on the money... the numbers... the dollar signs. The more you have, the more you think you need.

LOKISM #3

If you treat money like a drug, you're likely to become an addict.

If you put a group of millionaires in a room and ask them, "How many of you need more money?" every single hand will go up.

Even if you ask the same question with billionaires, everybody's hand would go up. They might say, "Well, even though I have enough money, I'm pursuing more because I'm just keeping score." Well, that's an excuse—in fact, it's the same excuse I used to make. But when does it end? When is enough really enough? Who would ever want the words "I wish I had worked more" engraved on their tombstone?

By knowing your F.U. Money amount and understanding YOUR target and YOUR ideal lifestyle, you will be able to avoid this mistake. You will be able to accomplish what you want to accomplish and achieve the ultimate freedom.

That's what this book is about: to make as much money as you damn well want, then live YOUR life—not anybody else's version of your life—as you damn well please. F.U. Money is truly the point of true liberation. F.U. Money is also a state of mind, a way of thinking, a belief. And most importantly, it's a way of living. It's when you get to the point that you are truly free.

Most people rarely do what they really want to do. That's why people go to work in jobs every day that they hate. That's why they stay with spouses they don't love anymore. That's why they go to places they don't want to go.

LOKISM #4

Most people don't do what they really want to do. They do what someone else wants them to do.

A LIFE OF REGRET AND DISAPPOINTMENT

Just think of how your life will be if you DON'T have F.U. Money. You'll say to yourself when you're ready to leave Planet Earth, "I wish I could have... I wish I would have..."

Instead, why not just say what William Hung said on American Idol:

"I already gave my best and I have no regrets at all."

Think about it. Why not enjoy life NOW?

When you have money pressures, you think about money all the time. You think, "How do I pay the bills?" and "How do I pay for my kid's education?"

LOKISM #5

Money is like sex. You'll think of nothing else if you don't have it—yet you're free to think of other things if you do have it.

When you don't have enough money, you're forced to say NO to opportunities with friends when they say, "Let's go on vacation together!" You say NO cause you can't afford it or you have to work. You'll say NO to charities because you don't have enough to give.

When I was broke, I wanted to give to the Children's Hospital because they saved my cousin's life. I was very grateful for the work that they had done, and I wanted to give them money—but I couldn't, because at the time I couldn't afford it. I couldn't even pay my own bills. I was struggling to just put food on the table.

You see, a lot of people say they want to help other people, but the truth is, they DON'T really want to help. How the hell can you help others if you don't help yourself first?

It's the old airplane/oxygen metaphor: you must first put on your own oxygen mask before helping others put theirs on. You have to save yourself first before you save the world. If you really want to help other people, make your F.U. Money. Then you can help whomever you want. The best way to help the poor is not to become one of them.

When you're constantly thinking about money, you are consumed by it. You focus on surviving—just paying the bills. A starving person can't think of anything beyond the gnawing in his belly. It's tough to be generous when you're broke. It's tough to think about other people's needs when your utilities are about to be turned off.

Some people say to me, "Dan you're so addicted... so obsessed with making money. All you care about is money."

Yes and no.

I DO think money is extremely important. But what I care about isn't money—what I really care about is freedom.

Money gives you freedom to make choices. I am very clear about what I want and what I don't want in life. And what I want is the freedom to buy whatever I want, eat whatever I want, and go wherever I want. And freedom costs money.

With F.U. Money, I am talking about living life to the fullest—about having it all. If you don't know your F.U. Money amount, you're flying through life blindly. You're working day in and day out, thinking, "Wouldn't it be nice if I had a different life?" yet never bothering to put a plan together to actually achieve the life that you want. And before you know it, life is over.

MAKE YOUR F.U. MONEY AS SOON AS POSSIBLE

I'm not suggesting for one second that you spend the rest of your life in the pursuit of F.U. Money. In fact, I'm saying the opposite. I'm saying get this money thing out of the way NOW so that you can live the life you truly want to live—so you're not forced to put your life on hold because you're always thinking that you "don't have the money."

LOKISM #6

F.U. Money is about living your life on your own terms— according to your possibilities, not your limitations.

I used to think that when I made my F.U. Money I would start pursuing my dreams, and one of the dreams was to learn how to fly a plane. For years, I wanted to do that, and I would say to myself, "When I have my F.U. Money, I'll learn to fly."

But then I thought, "Why the hell wait?"

Why not do it NOW? Why not do what I love NOW? So I immediately signed up for some flying lessons and got my private pilot's license. And you know what? It's absolutely wonderful!

What I found is that doing so didn't negatively affect my pursuit of F.U. Money at all. If anything, it had the opposite effect. It got me there faster because I was recharged and revitalized like never before. Spending the money on flying lessons (even though I didn't have a lot of money at the time) allowed me to experience the thrill of doing something I always wanted to do. It turned out to be the catalyst I needed to "kick me into high gear" pursuing my F.U. money. Once I had tasted the freedom of living the F.U. Money lifestyle, I became unstoppable.

F.U.M.A.
F.U. MONEY ASSIGNMENTS

1. What does F.U. Money mean to you?

2. What does your life look like once you have your F.U. Money?
   (Please be as specific as possible.)

3. How does it feel when you've made your F.U. Money?
   (for example: peace of mind, stress-free, joy, etc.)

CHAPTER 2

HOW TO LIVE LIKE A HOLLYWOOD MOVIE STAR
EVEN IF YOU'RE NOT FAMOUS

Imagine living like a Hollywood movie star.

What house would you live in? What car would you drive (or would you have a chauffer drive you)? Where would you take your next holiday?

What are your wildest dreams?

Think about it.

You see, we don't actually want more money—what we want is the freedom that money can buy.

In this chapter, I'm going to talk about how you can live like a rock star even if you're not famous. Hell, you can do with it without even being a millionaire. The trick is to know the difference between what's supposed to bring you pleasure and what actually brings you pleasure.

It's about what you really want, not the ideas the media has sold you on what you should want.

Let me give you a quick example. A friend of mine who is a very successful entrepreneur owns eight sports cars: two Ferraris, one Aston Martin, two Porsches, one Mercedes, a Dodge Viper... and a motorcycle to boot.

So, of course, he had to build a garage just to fit all his toys. The thing is, he's so busy that most of his "toys" have less than three thousand miles on them. I'm not kidding. It's ridiculous.

To make matters worse, all he can talk about is the next car he's going to buy! He's working harder and harder just to buy more toys that he won't use. Sheeesh.

Now don't get me wrong—I like cars. I have a sports car and a luxury car. That's all I need. Besides, since I work from home, I really don't drive that much anyway. And when I do go out, it's mostly for fun.

It's funny—as much as I enjoy cruising around town in my sport car, I probably get more satisfaction and fulfillment from having a good conversation with a friend. One costs money, one is free. But again, that's just me.

Now, you may be tempted to think, "Dan, if you prefer free stuff, like having good conversations with a friend, then why do you need all that money?" Good question. And the answer is that it's the money that affords me the opportunity to have those conversations whenever, wherever, and however often or for as long as I choose.

Most people are obligated to fill their days by working nine to five, five to seven days a week for someone else. To have a good conversation with a friend, they are forced to do it on evenings or weekends (or risk doing it during business hours and getting caught by the boss).

I don't have to put up with that bullshit! I can call a friend any time during any given week and say, "How about we do lunch tomorrow, and then go hang out at the beach for a while (or throw a party, go jet skiing, fly a plane... whatever)?"

That's freedom. Since I've made my F.U. Money, I don't answer to anyone. I'm the boss.

That's the difference. I figure what exactly it is that brings me the greatest pleasure, and then determine how much pleasure it offers and what I am willing to pay for it. It all goes back to understanding what makes you tick.

I've discovered that when you've made your F.U. Money, you can spend most of your time paying attention to things that bring you the greatest pleasure like reading a book, traveling, or having a good conversation with a friend.

Plus, you can afford to pay almost any price for anything (however, after a certain price point, you're just paying for prestige rather than quality). You can live very well, enjoy all the luxuries you can ever imagine, and still have so much money left over that you don't know what to do with it all.

The best things in life are affordable, but they're not cheap. Quality is never cheap, but if you buy quality items selectively and use with care, you can enjoy a life as materially rich as a Hollywood movie star. Have you ever really sat down and thought about what you will do with the money once you make your F.U. Money?

YOU CAN'T HIT A TARGET YOU CAN'T SEE

To reach your goals, you have to know what your goals are in the first place. You need to have what I call F.U. Money Targets—or F.U.M.T.s. Here's an example of what your F.U.M.T.s might look like:

1. Getting a Mercedes
2. Quitting your job
3. Buying a vacation home
4. One-month vacation to Europe
5. Paying off your mortgage

Whatever the target might be, first you must calculate what kind of money it takes to hit it. You don't just think, "Well, I want to make millions of dollars, hopefully." Don't be vague. Calculate how much money you're really talking about, and then I'll show you a way to get there faster than you ever thought possible.

Here's an assignment: before moving on, answer the questions below and take the corresponding actions.

F.U.M.A.
F.U. MONEY ASSIGNMENTS

1. Describe the material things that interest you, i.e., things that you often think about and that "turn you on," e.g., cars, travel, real estate, clothing, gadgets. Make a list of all the F.U.M.T.s you want. When do you want to hit those targets? Be specific, and map out all your F.U.M.T.s and list how much they cost.

1. _____
2. _____
3. _____
4. _____
5. _____
6. _____
7. _____
8. _____
9. _____
10. _____
11. _____
12. _____
13. _____
14. _____
15. _____
16. _____
17. _____
18. _____
19. _____
20. _____

2. In order to live "comfortably" in the home you want, with the cars and other F.U.M.T.s you want, what does your annual income need to be?

_____

I'll give you an example of my own F.U.M.T. list, with the cost by each item. This list was written in January 2002. I've since hit ALL of these targets except the mansion.

I thought a mansion is what I wanted, but in reality, it's not what I wanted at all. It was just an ego thing. Since I figured it was what all rich people had, I should have one as well. Seriously, who the hell needs a butler that comes at the ring of a bell and a one-hundred-thousand-dollar monthly overhead? If I were to buy a mansion, I would be buying one just to look cool and impress other people. Once I made my F.U. Money, I found out I really don't need to impress others anymore. The only person I have to impress is myself.

In fact, I don't even own a house. Why? Because in my opinion, a house is a series of furnace and air conditioner problems, pest-control issues, insurance woes, cleaning problems, malfunctioning appliances, and electrical and plumbing breakdowns. I am not a plumber, electrician, or handyman—nor do I desire to be the employer of anyone who is.

Instead, I live in a luxury condo. I came from Hong Kong. I've been living in skyscrapers all my life, so I'm very comfortable with them—plus I like the view! It's cozy, comfortable, and most importantly requires virtually NO maintenance. I want a carefree and hassle-free life.

Now, if owning a gorgeous home is your dream, be my guest—go for it. I'm NOT saying it's a bad thing, it's just not for me. Again, it goes back to knowing what makes you tick.

I choose to live in Vancouver, B.C., because of its combination of cool urban living that's only minutes away from gorgeous rural land-scapes. In fact, I can honestly say that if I were forced to choose only ONE place to live on this Earth, it would be here. It's a great city.

Dan Lok's Personal F.U.M.T List:

Luxury Condo ($2 mil)

Mortgage @ 7% w/no money down ($13,306.05/month)	$159.672.60/year
Lease two sports cars	$36,000/year
Exotic vacation every 90 days @$10,000/per vacation	$40,000/year
52 fancy meals at $200 each	$10,400/year
Dance lessons once/week @ $75 each	$3,900/year
Name brand clothes @$3,000/month	$36,000/year
Home theater system	$10,000
Maid service @ $500/week	$26,000/year
Lavish Christmas	$20,000/year
Lavish birthday	$20,000/year
Personal chef for 5 meals/week @ $30/meal	$3,900/year
Personal trainer for 3x/week @$120/week	$7,800/year
2 concert tickets, once concert/month	$6,000/year
Charity–Children's Hospital	$50,000/year
52 spa treatments @$100/treatment	$5,200/year
Flight lesson and rental	$50,000/year
Limousine rides	$5,000/year
Random Bills	$50,000/year
Buy-whatever-I-want-money	$100,000/year
Total	**$639,872.60/year**

Note: Big stuff like cars and houses are flat-out costs.
Items like "personal chef" are estimated costs.

If you add up all the F.U.M.T.s I have, it's about $640,000 per year. That's the cost of my ultimate lifestyle.

You might say, "Holy shit, Dan! That's a lot of money!" and you would be right—it IS a lot of money compared to where you are now. But it's not tens of millions or even a million dollars, is it? Stay with me, because in a moment I'm going to show you a shortcut to get to this amount (or more), regardless of where you are now.

My point is this: most people will realize when they go through this exercise that they actually don't need as much money as they think to live like a rock star. You can live lavishly, with a very nice home—a vacation home, too—and it still won't cost as much as you think. In fact, as you can see, in a way, I have to "work" pretty hard to "get rid" of $639,000 a year! Living like this and unloading all this money actually takes effort.

Lokism #7

Definition of F.U. Money: Any amount of money allowing the infinite perpetuation of wealth necessary to maintain a desired lifestyle without needing employment or assistance from anyone.

You may look at this list and realize that you would be happy with a lot less. And isn't happiness what we ultimately want? You can have all the security and happiness you want. Most people might think of F.U. Money as "being enough money to be able to say fuck you to anybody on the planet."

It's a little more sophisticated than that.

The actual definition of F.U. Money is any amount of money allowing the infinite perpetuation of wealth necessary to maintain a DESIRED LIFESTYLE without needing employment or assistance from anyone.

The keyword is *desired lifestyle*. It's not just about the money. It's about lifestyle. And I'm going to show you a SLOW way and a FAST way to get there....

TWO PROVEN WAYS TO MAKE YOUR F.U. MONEY

The Slow Way: Build a Big Nest Egg

The slow way is the traditional way: building a big nest egg, slowly accumulating wealth over time that accumulates into a big lump sum by the time you retire. That's what most people think of when they think of F.U. Money.

So, using this way, if you have a ten-million-dollar net worth by the time you retire, and it's returning a 10 percent yield, it will provide you one hundred thousand dollars in annual income. Take away about $350,000 for federal, state, and local taxes and that leaves you with $650,000 in cash to do whatever the hell you want. (The amount of tax you pay depends on where you live and what kind of deductions you have.)

And that's the slow way. To get there, you have to invest your money over thirty to forty years—most likely into a mutual fund—and hopefully the stock market doesn't crash.

Net Worth	10% yields	Annual Spendable Cash (After 35% Tax)
$1 million	$100,000	$65,000
$2 million	$200,000	$130,000
$5 million	$500,000	$325,000
$10 million	$1,000,000	$650,000
$20 million	$2,000,000	$1,300,000
$50 million	$5,000,000	$3,250,000
$100 million	$10,000,000	$6,500,000

As we saw in the fall of 2008, the stock market CAN crash. There are no guarantees. You can work your ass off all your life, socking away as much as you can into a mutual fund, only to get screwed in the end! Here you are, waiting and waiting for three or four decades to finally get to live your F.U. Money lifestyle when you retire, and yet you end up with a fraction of what you thought you would have.

And that's assuming you actually put enough away to have a ten-million-dollar net worth. Most people don't put away anywhere near that much money for retirement. Instead, they may have one million dollars in wealth, but as you can see in the chart above, that will only yield sixty-five thousand dollars a year at a 10 percent return. Hardly enough for a family to live comfortably, and certainly not enough to live a F.U. Money lifestyle.

The FAST Way: Automated Income Vehicles

This is the way that I've done it—by creating an automated vehicle that generates income without consuming time. Not only is it a much faster way, it's a much more certain way to do it.

When your automated income vehicle pays for your expenses and supports your desired lifestyle, you've made your F.U. Money! In essence you can stop working—retire today—and the income generated by your income producing vehicles will completely pay for your LIFESTYLE.

Let me illustrate. To keep things simple, let's just forget taxes, the cost of running an automated business, and stuff like that for a moment.

Divide $650,000 by 365 days to get a daily cost of living: $1,780.82.

Now, when you look at it on a daily basis, that's not too bad now, is it?

But you might say, "Dan, that's still a lot of money!"

Okay. Then let's break it down into products sold. Let's say you have a website, and you're selling a ninety-seven-dollar product, making fifty dollars in profit per sale. All you have to do is make thirty-six sales per day. That's only 1.5 sales per hour.

You can have one website that makes thirty-six sales per day, or you can have two or three websites each making eighteen sales each. Or you could reach the same goal if you had a $197 product making one hundred dollars in profit at 17.8 sales a day.

Cash	Daily Income (Divide by 365 Days)	Selling $97 product ($50 profit)	Selling $197 product ($100 profit)
$65,000	$178.08	3.5 sales per day	1.7 sales per day
$130,000	$356.16	7.12 sales per day	3.5 sales per day
$325,000	$890.41	17.8 sales per day	8.9 sales per day
$650,000	$1,780.82	35.6 sales per day	17.8 sales per day
$1,300,000	$3,561.64	71.2 sales per day	35.6 sales per day
$3,250,000	$8,904.10	178 sales per day	89 sales per day
$6,500,000	$17,808.21	356 sales per day	178 sales per day

Can you see how this is much more achievable for the average person? Can you see how you can get there in a much, much shorter period of time? And even better, it's a much more certain plan than relying on the stock market and risk becoming another victim of circumstances that are largely beyond your control. You ARE in control of how much money you make, and how quickly.

The rest of this book is focused on how to do it the fast way. That's how I've done it and that's how I advise you to do it. You can make your F.U. Money not in decades but in a few short years, just like me.

Strange as it sounds, I can't wait to hear actual stories of people who are able to tell their bosses, jerk clients, whomever to fuck off as a result of reading F.U. Money.

part 2:

THE F.U.
MONEY
MYTHS

Eight Myths That
Are Keeping You
From Making
Your F.U. Money

CHAPTER 3

F.U. MONEY MYTH #1: MONEY CAN'T BUY HAPPINESS

Don't you just hate it when people tell you that money can't buy happiness? That is fucking bullshit. It's nonsense. If you don't think money can buy happiness, you don't know where to shop.

"Riches may not bring happiness, but neither does poverty."
- SOPHIE IRENE LOEB

Poverty only breeds misery and more poverty.

If you don't think money can buy happiness, you're living a lie that broke people came up with. I know a ton of people who are broke—and they are miserable because of it. I've been broke and I've been rich, and I can honestly say rich is a HELL of a lot better. Better to be a rich son of a bitch than a poor son of a bitch.

Money is fantastic. Money is GOOOOOD. I love making money because it gives you choices. It gives you freedom. It gives you control. It buys you time.

Money gives you the power to do the things you want to do when you want to do them. What could possibly be wrong with that?

Lokism #8

Money buys you time—and time translates to the freedom to pursue happiness and personal growth, the freedom to help others, and the freedom to do whatever you damn well please.

HOW ONE LATE-NIGHT PHONE CALL CHANGED MY LIFE FOREVER

I'll never forget. It was two a.m. on a Saturday. I was asleep and I barely heard the phone ring and ring and ring. Finally, I picked it up and half-asleep said, "This is Dan Lok."

I heard a woman's voice on other end saying, "Dan, this is your aunt."

I grumbled, "Uhh, who's this?"

"This is your aunt."

"Oh hey. What's… what's the occasion? What's happening?"

"Dan, your father just had a stroke."

"What!"

"Your father just had a stroke."

(Although my father and mother are divorced, I love him deeply. We don't see each other much since he's in Hong Kong and I'm in Canada.)

At that moment, it was like everything stopped. All the memories of my father and me flooded my mind with waves of flashbacks.

Tears started to fall as I began to cry and panic saying, "Is he okay? What happened?"

My aunt answered, "We don't know—he was with his friend and suddenly he just had a stroke. His friend took him to the hospital and now he's in the emergency room. The doctors are performing surgery. It looks like it's very serious. He might or might not make it."

I blurted out, "Oh my God, oh my God, what should I do?"

She said, "I'll call you right back."

I spent the next seven hours pacing the floor, staring at the phone, playing through all the worst-case scenario scenes in my head. Finally, the phone rang. I knew it was my aunt but I was terrified to answer it. I took a deep breath and picked up the telephone.

"Dan, your father is okay now, fortunately. The doctor said he is very lucky that his friend was with him when it happened. If he had arrived thirty minutes later at the hospital, he probably would not have made it."

I exhaled the deepest sigh of relief my lungs had ever breathed.

Then my aunt said to me, "Well, do you want to fly back and visit your father? He'll want to see you."

And at that point, I was forced to admit ashamedly to my aunt, "I really want to, but I just can't afford it. I just don't have the money." I was so broke. I was barely surviving on minimum wage. Worse, I was deeply in debt.

I wanted to ask them to loan me the thousands of dollars it would cost for a plane ticket to Hong Kong. I finally talked to my father, and he said, "Son, don't worry. I'm okay. You don't need to fly back." He was just saying that to comfort me. He wanted to see me, I knew it. And I desperately wanted to see him—yet, I couldn't.

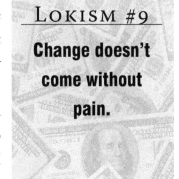

LOKISM #9

Change doesn't come without pain.

At that moment, I became 100 percent committed to the decision that I would NEVER again be a slave to money. Fuck that! I would no longer let money control my life or allow it to be the thing that decides what I can and can't do.

Instead, I would make my F.U. Money. I would take control of my financial situation and make so much damn money that I would never have to go through this painful experience again.

Some people say money is not that important. Tell that to the family who's starving right now, or to the family who needs serious medical help. They'll tell you how important money is.

We have been conditioned since childhood to believe that wanting money is wrong and unethical. Yet the entire world seems to run on money.

Just look around you at the countries or even cities that lack money. What do you find at these places? Usually more crime being committed, more people taking advantage of others, more disease, more suffering, more death, and none or very little education.

LOKISM #10

Money is the root of all good.

Money may not be the most important thing in life, but let's face it: money is pretty damn important in this day and age. Money can buy food, clothing, warmth, and shelter—if you know how to be happy without those things, let me know.

Love doesn't pay the rent. Love doesn't put food on your plate. Love doesn't keep you warm in the midst of winter. Love doesn't provide financial security for retirement. Love can't buy the operation your mother needs. Love can't pay for your child's education.

It's money that does ALL these things. Money is the root of ALL GOOD.

F.U.M.A.
F.U. MONEY ASSIGNMENTS

Complete the following phrases quickly and without thinking. Don't censor anything you think or anything you write down. Write whatever comes to your mind.

1. Money is _____

2. Money is _____

3. Money is _____

4. Money is _____

5. Money is _____

6. My father thought money was _____

7. My mother thought money was _____

8. In my family, money caused _____

9. My friends think money _____

10. Having money is not _____

11. In order to have money, I'd have to _____

Answer the following questions to help you uncover your negative beliefs about money.

1. What did you discover regarding your beliefs about money? What do you believe it takes to make your F.U. Money?

2. Why do you believe these things now? What evidence have you seen in your life to prove to you that these beliefs are true for you?

3. How does it serve you to keep believing this? What price do you pay by continuing to believe this?

4. How does believing this prevent you from making your F.U. Money?

Chapter 4

F.U. MONEY MYTH #2: RICH PEOPLE ARE ASSHOLES

The media loves to point out that "rich people are assholes." Why do they say this?

Because it makes poor people feel better about themselves.

Don't believe what you hear from the media. Why not find out for yourself? The majority of wealthy people I know are some of the nicest, happiest, most generous people I know. I challenge you to get out there and actually meet some of them and see if you find out differently. I don't think you will.

My mentor said to me years ago, "Sure, there are rich people who commit suicide, but I'm damn sure there are a lot more poor people who kill themselves than rich people."

Now, are there some rich assholes? Sure, there are rich people who are assholes, just like there are poor people who are assholes. The character of a person has nothing to do with whether she is rich or poor.

AREN'T RICH PEOPLE MEAN AND GREEDY?

If you actually meet some rich people, you'll find out they give back. They give to charities and often have businesses that provide for communities in terms of providing jobs, as well as tax revenue for the city and state.

How can they do it? Because they aren't thinking ONLY about themselves. Since they have more than enough, they CAN think about other people and therefore make a difference in the lives of many. Rich people who use their wealth for the betterment of others can accomplish so much more, which brings even more success and happiness in other areas.

Think about it. Look at Bill Gates—now you can say whatever you want about him, that Microsoft is a monopoly, that he's greedy, that he's "crushing small business" and taking over the world—whatever.

I dare you to try to find anyone who has been MORE charitable than Bill Gates. In the years since Microsoft went public, Gates has donated billions of dollars to charities. I guess the only one more charitable would be Warren Buffet. He gives away 97 percent of his net worth—billions and billions of dollars!

There are poor people who will STILL criticize these men. They feel justified in their stupidity by saying, "Hell, they're RICH! They SHOULD give their money away."

So, instead, I want to know—what the HELL have poor people done for society lately? Nothing! Why? Because they can't afford to do anything! And yet they try to sit in judgment of those who ARE doing something because they CAN. People are fucking nuts.

I've found that it's the same poor people, who sit in judgment of rich people like this, that have a welfare mentality.

Poor people have a sense of entitlement. They think the world owes them something. They are selfish as hell.

These same people wouldn't be caught dead reading a book like this, acquiring new knowledge and trying to improve their miserable lives. They're the same people who wouldn't set foot in a public library if their lives depended on it (a place where they could LEARN SKILLS to improve their financial situation—for FREE!)

They're living paycheck-to-paycheck, and yet they still would rather spend every last penny on junk food, video games, romance novels, cigarettes, and illegal drugs. They waste their time watching Jerry Springer reruns on TV and surfing porn on the Internet.

In fact, it's been my experience that it's poor people who have lied, cheated, and stolen from me throughout the years.

They are the salesmen trying to sell me crap I don't need. The con-artists who try to rip me off when I go to get my car fixed. The lazy employees who surf the Internet and work as little as possible when the boss isn't looking. The Medicaid recipients who clog up emergency rooms when they have a slight case of the sniffles or a headache—and force healthcare costs to skyrocket for everyone else.

Now, are ALL poor people lazy and are ALL rich people generous? Of course not. Just don't let the media brainwash you. Why not find out yourself what rich people are really like? Go and talk to some of them.

LOKISM #12

Banks don't get robbed by those of us pulling up in a limousine or Rolls Royce.

WON'T MONEY CHANGE WHO I AM?

I get another excuse from people all the time, "Dan, I'm afraid that money will change who I am." What kind of stupid thought is that? Let's get real for a moment.

Let me tell you something: money only makes a good man better and a bad man worse.

Money is neutral—it's paper. It's just a medium of exchange—nothing more, nothing less. It doesn't possess some evil power that can change who you are. It's not magical. It's not going to change your core being. It won't change who you are—and if it does, there's something seriously wrong with you. Money simply amplifies more of what you are. If you're a jerk, more money will just make you a bigger jerk. If you're a nice person, more money will make you a nicer person.

LOKISM #13

If you're a jerk, more money will just make you a bigger jerk. If you're a nice person, more money will make you a nicer person.

A man approaches a beautiful woman in a bar and without any small talk, asks her, "If I give you a dollar, would you sleep with me?"

The woman instantly becomes angry, slaps him, and snarls, "Absolutely NOT!"

Before she gets away, he asks her second question, "Well then, would you sleep with me for a million dollars?"

The woman pauses, thinks about it for a second, and then says, "Yes, I would."

Then the man responds, "How about for twenty bucks?"

Again, the woman looks angry and says, "Of course not! What kind of woman do you think I am?"

The man replies, "We've already settled on what kind of woman you really are, we're just negotiating the price."

F.U.M.A.
F.U. MONEY ASSIGNMENTS

Complete the following phrases quickly and without thinking. Don't censor anything you think or anything you write down. Write whatever comes to your mind.

1. Rich people are _____

2. Rich people are _____

3. Rich people are _____

4. Poor people are _____

5. Poor people are _____

6. Poor people are _____

7. Being broke tells me_____

8. Being rich tells me_____

Answer the following questions to help you uncover your negative beliefs about rich people.

1. What did you discover regarding your beliefs about money? What do you believe it takes to make your F.U. Money?

2. Why do you believe these things now? What evidence have you seen in your life to prove to you that these beliefs are true?

3. How does it serve you to keep believing this? What price do you pay by continuing to believe this?

4. How does believing this prevent you from making your F.U. Money?

CHAPTER 5

F.U. MONEY MYTH #3: YOU CAN AFFORD TO WAIT

Think you have forever? Think again!

Let's say the average lifespan is seventy years. For the first twenty years of your life you're growing up. Your parents are taking care of you while you learn to be an adult—you're a kid.

You really don't have a lot of choices while you're living with your parents. So the first twenty years are gone, now you have fifty years left. So at twenty you're an adult. You can make choices and decide what it is you want to do.

One third of your life is spent sleeping. The other one third of that is wasted on entertainment, relaxing, watching TV, having sex, going to the bathroom, commuting to and from work, etc.

When you really crunch the numbers, you really only have ten or fifteen years to work with and make your F.U. Money.

And that ten or fifteen years doesn't even count the mistakes you'll make, the financial setbacks you'll have, or the learning curve you'll have to go through. Now do you see why "get rich slow" doesn't work?

WHO THE HELL SAID IT WAS A GOOD IDEA TO RETIRE AT SIXTY-FIVE?

Why would you want to wait until you're sixty-five to retire? Who came up with that crap anyway? The government? Oh, sure. The government sure has your best interest at heart, huh?

Why not make your F.U. Money and retire as quickly as possible, and then not have to work unless you want to? Why wait until sixty-five? Why not fifty-five or forty-five or thirty-five?

LOKISM #14

Making huge sums of money consistently requires a set of skills.

You can develop the ability to create money out of thin air. I know that sounds far-fetched, but true freedom comes when you have developed the skills, the creativity, and the mindset that it's the fruit of your hard work and creativity that provides financial security.

The reward is not only the money—that's part of it—but also knowing you have the confidence, the freedom, and the ability to make money whenever you need to.

"The real source of wealth and capital in this new era is not material things. It is the human mind, the human spirit, the human imagination, and our faith in the future."

-STEVE FORBES, BILLIONAIRE PUBLISHER

Like I said, F.U. Money is NOT just a number. It's a way of thinking. It's a mindset and a way of acting—a behavioral pattern. It's a way of life that allows you to make a lot of money and not have to wait until you're sixty-five to enjoy it.

Let me ask you… Do you want to travel the world? If you said YES, would you like to do it when you're sixty-five or when you're forty-five?

THE TWO MOST IMPORTANT QUESTIONS YOU CAN ASK YOURSELF EVERY DAY

How long did it take for me to make my F.U. Money? I consider myself a seven-year "overnight success." In other words, it took me seven years to make my F.U. Money—but when it happened, it happened rapidly.

This is pretty common. Everybody hits a time in their lives when they accomplish more in twelve months than in the past twelve years. The key is to make sure that YOUR productive one-year period is going to allow you to make your F.U. Money.

To do so, you must immerse yourself in the mindset of wealth creation. That's the difference. It's why most millionaires get started slowly but get rich on a fast break at some point in their lives.

They sleep, eat and spend their time thinking, "How can I make my F.U. Money as quickly as humanly possible?" They take every action into account. They constantly ask themselves, "What have I done today that will move me closer to my F.U. Money?"

* Go to www.fumoney.com/freegifts for a printable copy of the "Lokisms" Wall Poster. It is a great way to "immerse yourself" in the F.U. Money philosophies. Th is poster contains all the "Lokisms" in this book so you can print them out and post them on your wall.

F.U.M.A.
F.U. MONEY ASSIGNMENTS

1. How many years from now do you want to make your F.U. Money?

2. Brainstorm at least five things you can do this week that will move you closer to your F.U. Money.

1. _____

2. _____

3. _____

4. _____

5. _____

CHAPTER 6

F.U. MONEY MYTH #4: YOU HAVE TO BE LUCKY

Lotteries are for suckers. They're a cunning way for state politicians to siphon money right out of the pockets of their constituents—without adding new taxes.

When you play the lottery, it's like giving free money to your state government. (Hell, you would be better off just mailing a check to your state representative; at the least you might get a thank-you letter.)

Most people know it's a long shot to win the lottery, but they don't have any idea how long of a shot it really is. According to SavingAdvice.com, single state lotteries usually have odds of about eighteen million to one, and multiple state lotteries have odds as high as 120 million to one.

Therefore…

- You are six to forty-five times more likely to die from a lightning strike than you would be to win the lottery.
- You are eighteen to 120 times more likely to die from flesh-eating bacteria than to win the lottery.

- You're 180 to 1,200 times more likely to die from snake bite or bee sting than win the lottery.
- You are 30,000 to 200,000 percent more likely to die in a legal execution than to win the lottery.
- According to Space.com, you are 450,000 to three million times more likely to die in an asteroid collision in the year 2029 than to win the lottery.
- If you drive ten miles to purchase your lottery ticket, it's three to twenty times more likely for you to be killed in a car accident along the way than to win the jackpot.

Needless to say, I've never bought a lottery ticket in my life! I don't believe in getting rich through luck.

WHY LOTTERIES ARE MAGNETS FOR LAZY AND STUPID PEOPLE

It amazes me that poor people can read story after story of rags-to-riches millionaires (not sports stars or celebrities, but real stories of "average" people who made it big) and yet still tell themselves, "The only way I'll ever get rich is by winning the lottery."

Bottom line, people who think this way are either lazy or stupid or both. Am I being too harsh? I don't think so.

Think about this scenario. A rich person could say, "I was a dirt-broke auto mechanic who was one hundred thousand in debt, but then I went to a seminar and learned how to start an Internet business. Five years later, I am a millionaire."

A smart person would think, "I wonder what seminar he went to? How did he do it? I wonder if I could learn to do that."

A stupid person would think, "Internet sounds complicated. I could never do that." He wouldn't think about the fact that if a former auto mechanic was able to learn how to do it, he could probably learn to do it, too.

A lazy person, upon hearing this same story would make excuses like, "But that guy probably sits in front of a computer all day. I'm not a computer geek, you know."

Truth is, a lazy person would rather make excuses why she can't do something than to bother investigating how she could possibly do it herself.

So instead, lazy and stupid people will continue to play the lottery and keep dreaming (with their other lazy and stupid friends) about what they would do with the money if they won.

Being lazy and stupid is far worse than being broke. Being lazy and stupid is pretty much the lowest you can fall. If you're broke but you have information and you're willing to change, then you're not going to stay broke for long.

WHY LOTTERY WINNERS GO BANKRUPT

According to the Certified Financial Planners Board of Standards, one-third of lottery winners eventually declare bankruptcy. How does this happen?

Since lottery winners make their F.U. Money by accident, the financial security offered lottery winners is an illusion.

They never acquire the F.U. Money mindset and skill sets they need to put their money to good use. Eventually, most lottery winners will blow all the money they win on nonsense and still go broke. Some even commit suicide.

Why does this happen? Because they relied on luck alone to get the money. Luck wasn't enough to carry them into the future and assure that they would stay rich. To do that, it takes intelligence.

WHY MAKING YOUR F.U. MONEY HAS VERY LITTLE TO DO WITH LUCK

Making your F.U. Money has very little to do with luck. Instead, it has everything to do with your talent, skills, ability, and knowledge… and that's the good news for you and me!

The fact is, if getting rich only occurred when people got lucky, then we would all be fucked. Books like the one you're reading right now wouldn't be necessary.

Let me ask you this: Can you develop new moneymaking skills? How about improving your business acumen? Can you acquire new knowledge?

That's why investing in yourself is the smartest decision you can ever make. You are the only one who can control you. When you make the decision that you WILL learn how to make your F.U. Money, and you WILL apply what you learn, there's simply no limit to what you can achieve.

It simply never occurs to most people that they can do this. They sit and watch other people get rich, never asking themselves, "How could I learn to do that?"

STRIP AWAY ALL MY MONEY AND I'LL MAKE IT ALL BACK… 100 PERCENT GUARANTEED

If I lose everything tomorrow, I know I could make it all back. How can I be so damn sure? Because this has already happened to me… twice!

I've been financially dead TWICE in my life. Once I was even on the edge of filing bankruptcy and my friends and family saved my ass. Yet I came back. I learned from my mistakes; I got up off the ground and dusted myself off.

I made my money by design in the first place—I didn't make it by accident. Once you gain the knowledge on how to get rich, you never lose it! Now, that is true financial security.

So forget about money falling into your lap. It's time to get real. Roll up your sleeves and get to work improving your talent, skills, ability, and knowledge.

LOKISM #15

You don't just get rich. You must earn the right to be rich.

CHAPTER 7

F.U. MONEY MYTH #5: YOU HAVE TO BE A CHEAPSKATE

Financial gurus always talk about living on a budget. I say the hell with a budget! Spend the money. Enjoy life NOW. What are you saving it for anyway?

Think I'm full of it? Let me tell you a true story about my friends, Mike and Andrea.

Just three years ago, Mike was earning forty thousand dollars a year as a salesperson for a company that supplies food to restaurants. His wife Andrea

> ### LOKISM #16
> **It's easier to make MORE money than it is to spend less.**

worked part-time earning about ten thousand dollars a year. The rest of the time she spent raising their young kids. Every month they struggled to pay their bills.

Desperately seeking help, they attended a "financial workshop" at their church taught by a well-known so-called financial "guru." This "expert" told them that the only way they were going to get ahead was to cut back on spending and put themselves on a tighter budget.

They were told that they should only drive used cars, and to never buy those "expensive coffee drinks at Starbucks." They were supposed to take what little money they could save and put it into mutual funds so they could earn 10 percent interest on their savings. They would be able to safely retire at sixty-five with a few million in the bank.

"Something just rubbed me wrong with this line of thinking," said Mike. "It all just seemed so focused on limitations, scarcity, and being cheap for the rest of my life. That's not how I want to live."

Instead, Mike took a hard look at what he was doing to make money in the first place. At the particular company he worked for, top salespeople made around one hundred thousand a year, and it often took five to ten years to reach this point.

Then he noticed something about the top salespeople that bothered him. He told me, "I realized they had as many customers placing orders on Monday as I had all week."

It dawned on him that even though these top performers were making what sounded to him at the time like big money, "they were working their asses off."

To make the "big" money, the top salespeople were constantly working seventy-hour weeks and dealing with stressful situations that inevitably came as a result of having so many accounts. Mike finally realized that being a top salesperson at this company wasn't worth the hassle, so he started looking elsewhere.

He'd always been interested in marketing, so he thought about going back to college to earning a marketing degree. "The counselor basically sat me down and talked me out of it," he laughs. "He showed me how it would take me five long years of going to night school and a total hardship on my family life. Plus, even when I graduated, I would have no guarantee of making over seventy-five thousand dollars a year. And it would have taken me years just to pay off the student loans."

He was still at a loss for what to do—that is, until he had a fateful conversation with one of his restaurant customers. He confided in his customer that he was really interested in marketing, and that was the moment the customer gave him an audiotape that changed Mike's life forever.

This customer said that she had gone to a food show and heard this guy give a presentation in which he talked about unique marketing techniques for restaurants. Apparently this "marketing guru" was mailing these crazy long sales letters to get catering jobs for his own restaurant, and as a result he was blowing the doors off his competition.

"I listened to that tape at least ten times," Mike said. "I was completely fascinated that someone could mail out a long letter that was basically a sales presentation, and it would actually get new customers to call him." As a salesperson, Mike had only known two ways of getting customers, and that was "pounding the pavement" (cold-calling door to door), or "dialing for dollars" (making cold calls on the phone). Mike went on to study all of this marketing guru's materials and began to research others who used similar techniques.

Today, just three years later, Mike and Andrea both work from home, working as direct response marketing copywriters, writing long-form sales letters for businesses of all types. They have a waiting list of at least six weeks. In fact, they have so much business that they are now starting to outsource to other copywriters. "We will easily earn over $250,000 this year with our copywriting business," he says.

The amazing thing is Mike and Andrea didn't have to go to college to learn this valuable skill. "We bought a course for $1,500 that told us exactly what to do. We started making good money within a couple months. We've raised our prices about five times in the last two years, but our customers keep coming back and referring others to us. We don't spend a penny on advertising."

Plus, they work from home and take off whenever they want. "Every now and then I'll go to a restaurant and see a salesperson doing my old job. When I do, I pray silently and thank God that I'm not doing that anymore!"

A PENNY SAVED IS SILL JUST A PENNY

"Waste not, want not. Be tight, be frugal. Cut up your credit cards. Live below your means. Don't drink the latte coffee in the morning. Save that few dollars."

> LOKISM #17
>
> **Focus on generating dollars, not pinching pennies.**

"A penny saved is a penny earned." BULLSHIT. A penny saved is still just a fucking penny.

You see, Mike and Andrea succeeded because they made a choice NOT to scrimp and save. They said, "The HELL with that!"

Instead, they decided to change their financial situation by learning a new high-paying skill. And what's even better, they didn't learn this skill by going to college: they simply bought a copywriting course for $1,500 and just started doing it. I love it!

Mike and Andrea have been freed up to live life they want NOW, while they're young. They go on three or four vacations per year, not only because they have the money but also because they don't have to answer to some asshole boss telling them when they can or can't go on vacation! If they want to go, they just GO.

That's how YOU should live. You should be able to buy stuff you want to buy and go where you want to go, as long as your cash flow will support it.

Here's the thing that most people will never understand: you will not become a mega- millionaire until you begin to think and live like one.

Now, I am NOT talking about living off credit cards or borrowed money. I am NOT talking about spending foolishly either. You should buy whatever you want as your income grows, as long as the gap keeps getting larger. Does that make sense? Isn't that why we work so hard anyway? To buy the things that give us pleasure?

No matter where you live, I'm sure you've met people that complain about the price of food, gas prices, or electricity bills, etc. Here's my advice—don't worry about it because there isn't a damn thing you can do about it anyway.

Besides, why worry about things you can't control? What you can control is changing your financial situation. When you get to the point where you're making more than you spend, crap like how much food costs won't matter anymore.

I LOVE MY CREDIT CARDS

One of the credit cards I have is the TD First Class Travel Visa Infinite that I use to save up travel points. I get a lot of points I could use for free traveling, so I love using the credit card and buying expensive stuff.

I have zero credit card debt. I pay off my balance every single month. I love using my credit cards. There's absolutely nothing wrong with spending money.

Instead of cutting up your credit cards, living below your means, and always feeling poor, make your F.U. Money. Buy whatever you damn well want as long as the cash flow from your businesses and investments supports it.

When you make a lot of money and you're only spending 15 to 20 percent of your income, suddenly the budgeting is just not that important now, is it?

Besides, why make it if you're not going to spend it? What are you saving it for? Till you die? To pass on to your heirs?

WHY SAVING YOUR WAY TO THE F.U. MONEY SUCKS

Am I telling you not to save money? Hell no. Because if you don't, you won't have money to invest, to grow and start businesses, and be ready when opportunities come along that require some money. I'm not saying that.

What I am saying is, why not enjoy the journey while pursuing your F.U. Money? Don't sweat the small stuff. If your time is spent pinching pennies, it can't be focused on generating dollars. If you generate enough dollars, the pennies won't matter.

Don't you know some people who are just cheap as hell? What do they look like?

You can just see it in their faces. They're not happy. They're depressed because they're hanging on to every penny they have. They clip coupons, drive miles out of their way to get cheaper gasoline and line up at the crack of dawn for special sales. They won't even go out to dinner with friends because they're trying to save a couple bucks. Bottom line: they don't enjoy life.

Money is just a vehicle, a medium to get you what you want. So you shouldn't sacrifice your life, your fulfillment, and your enjoyment just because you want to save a few measly bucks.

Even when I was struggling financially, to condition myself for wealth (and NOT for poverty) I would go to a five-star hotel, grab a cup of coffee or tea (which was about all I could afford), and sit in the lobby. I would "loiter" in the hotel and just immerse myself in that environment.

LOKISM #18

Most people save their way to bankruptcy.

When I had to go the airport, instead of taking a cab from my house, which is what most people do, I would take a limousine.

Now, do you think there's a difference when you arrive in a limousine versus a cab? You bet there is. There's a huge difference. When you're riding in a limousine, people look at you and say, "Wow, he must be important." Again, I was training myself to get comfortable with the F.U. Money lifestyle.

And here's the thing: a limousine actually doesn't cost that much more that a cab. From my place to the airport for a cab, it's fifty bucks. If I take a limo (a stretch limo, by the way, not the short one, the long one), I'm talking about less than ninety-five bucks, so a little less than double.

Now, was it necessary for me to spend that extra money? No. But what I wanted to do was condition my mind to get comfortable with having my F.U. Money. I wanted to condition my mind that I deserve these great things, that I deserve better things in life.

A LESSON I LEARNED FROM FRANK SINATRA

If you were to hang out with me for a while, you'd quickly realize that I am not cheap. Frank Sinatra's custom was to leave a tip of one hundred dollars for good service. And that was back when one hundred bucks could actually buy something.

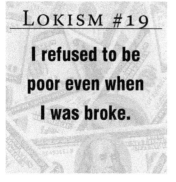

LOKISM #19

I refused to be poor even when I was broke.

So, if I'm eating in a restaurant and I like the waiter or waitress's service, I always over-tip, sometimes up to 30 percent of my meal cost. I don't do this just because I have a lot of money. I did this even when I didn't have a lot of money. And back then, the restaurants I used to go to were just as fancy and expensive as where I go now.

When I get good service, I feel like I should pay for it. Why? Because even when I didn't have a lot of money, I still thought like a rich person. I absolutely refused to be a cheap bastard. I have always believed there's plenty to go around. There's plenty for me and for everybody else. I can always make more money.

F.U.M.A.

F.U. MONEY ASSIGNMENTS

Complete the following phrases quickly and without thinking. Don't censor anything you think or anything you write down. Write whatever comes to your mind.

1. If I could afford it, I'd _____

2. If I could afford it, I'd _____

3. If I could afford it, I'd _____

4. If I weren't so cheap, I'd _____

5. If I weren't so cheap, I'd _____

6. If I weren't so cheap, I'd _____

7. I'm afraid that if I didn't save money, I'd _____

8. I'm afraid that if I didn't save money, I'd _____

9. I'm afraid that if I didn't save money, I'd _____

CHAPTER 8

F.U. MONEY MYTH #6: YOU HAVE TO GET RICH SLOW

Whenever I'm speaking at a conference, when I throw out the phrase "get rich quick" the negative reaction from the audience is obvious.

Every face in the audience has this look on it like, "No, no, you CAN'T get rich quick."

Every one of us has it ingrained into our psyche that if it sounds too good to be true, it probably is. Any idea that even remotely hints at "get rich quick" MUST be some sort of scam.

Let me ask you a question, if you're going to get rich, isn't it your choice to do it at any given rate of "speed" that you want? Do you get bonus points if you get rich slowly? Is there anything wrong if you make it quickly?

WHO GETS RICH QUICK?

Now you may be thinking, "Who gets rich quick?" I'm NOT talking about first-round draft pick athletes who sign on to multimillion dollar contracts, or pop stars who get "discovered" and find themselves suddenly famous. These kinds of people are so few and far-between, it's almost like winning the lottery.

This is not a "model" that can be followed by the average person. Unfortunately, since "famous" people like this are usually the only ones who draw media attention, the average person believes that these are the only types of people who "legitimately" get rich quick. Not true.

I personally know thousands and thousands of "average" people who went from rags to riches in a short period of time. How did they do it?

Many made their fortune in businesses. Some made their fortune in the stock market. Others made it in real estate. The story of how they did it varies with every single person. The thing to remember is that it does happen.

Unlike famous athletes or pop stars who have natural talents and skills that most of us will never have, these lesser known rags-to-riches folks are better role models for all of us since what they have achieved can be repeated by "average" people.

LOKISM #20

Money is attracted to speed.

Copy someone who's making a fortune right now. Read about them, talk to them if you can, and emulate them. Success leaves clues. You CAN follow in the footsteps of success and become successful yourself! (In fact, it's the most certain way to do it.)

WHY GET RICH SLOW DOESN'T WORK

"Get rich slow" is ridiculous—yet you're being "sold" this very concept everywhere you look. Some morons somewhere came up with the idea that the only way the "average" person could ever hope to "legitimately" get rich was to do it slowly.

Bookstores and libraries are filled to the brim with financial books that tell you to invest your money little by little and let the miracle of compound interest do its "magic."

So, in other words, if you invest a little bit of money every month, then in ten, twenty, or thirty years, you will have accumulated millions of dollars because of the miracle of compound interest—and someday decades from now, you will make your F.U. Money.

These financial advisors talk about getting rich on your existing income level. They want you to save, live below your means, invest 10 percent of your income into a mutual fund or pension, and in thirty years, VOILA… you'll be rich.

So they basically want you to be POOR all of your life so you can somehow be RICH the last few years you're here on this planet—when you're old and sick. It's just fucking insane. Does that sound like a good plan to you? Putting off your hopes and dreams until you've worked forty years?

Be honest with me here, is that what you really want, or is that what you've been told that you should want?

Here's a fact: out of the hundreds of millionaires and multimillionaires I know (even a handful of billionaires I've met), I don't know anybody that actually got rich this way. I don't anybody who actually made their F.U. Money like this.

Not even ONE.

Sure, compound interest sounds good in theory, but very few people have the discipline and the patience to wait thirty or forty years to get rich. I know I sure don't! It's unrealistic. I'm sure there are some people out there who have the discipline to do it, I just haven't met a single one of them myself.

WHY PLAYING IT SAFE IS ONLY THE ILLUSION OF SAFETY

We've been taught practically since birth that the "goal" of our existence should be to go to school and get a good job so we can retire at sixty-five years old. That's supposed to be the "safe" thing to do, right? Guess again.

The other day I saw an old lady working at McDonald's. Here she is in her "Golden Years" working under the "Golden Arches." Why? Who knows? Maybe her husband died early, and she didn't have the means to make ends meet. Maybe she doesn't have the skills to work for anything more than minimum wage.

As baby boomers age, more and more are finding out the hard way that they just don't have enough money to retire. Although they want to stop working and enjoy the retirement they always dreamed of, they can't. So much for "traveling the world" when you have to clock in at Wal-Mart every day just to survive!

To make matters worse, their cost of living keeps increasing—gas prices, heating oil, food prices, prescriptions—the list goes on and on. Yet earning power as baby boomers age decreases. By that point, there's not a lot they can do about it, at least not in the traditional working world.

And to make matters even worse, even the boomers who were "prepared" have had their retirement dreams crushed in this latest stock market crash. A friend of mine who contributed savings to his retirement fund month after month, year after year, had his entire lifetime savings wiped out by the failing of Lehman Brothers. Just like that—his entire life savings was GONE.

All because of some greedy Wall Street bankers playing fast and loose with risky investments, my friend has seen his dream retirement go up in smoke. He told me, "Dan, I honestly have NO idea what I'm going to do now. All my money is GONE."

Maybe you're reading this and you, too, saw your 401(k) get cut in half (or worse) in this latest stock fiasco. Or maybe you saw it happen to your parents or someone else you know.

The lesson should be clear: safety is an illusion. There is no such thing as a "safe job." There is NO "secure pension" that you can rely on in your Golden Years. Betting it all on a 401(k) with no "Plan B" is borderline suicidal.

The only "sure thing" you can bet on is you. Here's what I mean: when you place your hopes and dreams of retirement in the hands of your job, a pension plan, a spouse, or a 401(k) plan, you're basically putting control in the hands of other people. Control is out of your hands.

When instead you say, "If it's gonna be, it's up to me," you take control of your financial destiny. You begin to think differently about educating yourself. You start to look at risk differently. All of a sudden, starting a business of your own doesn't seem so "risky" after all. In fact, it will look more and more like the SAFE thing to do. That's because it IS.

HOW THE RICH REALLY GET RICH

As I've said, all the millionaires and multimillionaires I know personally have made their F.U. Money either through businesses or investments—most of the time a combination of both. AND most of them made their money in a short period time (three to seven years), not necessarily a long period of time (thirty to forty years).

Here's what works:

1. Dramatically increase your income.
2. Own a business that allows you to leverage other people's time, knowledge, and energy so you make money while you sleep.
3. Invest that excess cash into high growth investments.

That's how I've done it. That's how a lot of rich people have done it. NOT all of them, but a lot of them. That's the RIGHT way. That's the smart way.

LOKISM #21

Rich people are entrepreneurs who invest.

GET RICH QUICK OR GET RICH SLOW?

So, if you have the choice (and you do), why the hell would you want to get rich slow? Why would you NOT want to get rich quick?

Now let's get something straight: when I say "get rich quick" I'm not talking about buying into some kind of scheme where you plug your money into a so-called "once-in-a-lifetime opportunity" that's really some unproven (or possibly even illegal) "trick" supposed to get some kind of crazy high return on investment. That's called being an idiot. That's NOT what I am talking about.

I'm talking about improving yourself, developing the skill set and the business acumen to become a person who is worthy of wealth—a person who has the ability to generate wealth very quickly. That's what I'm talking about.

LOKISM #22

You can't be a millionaire with fifty-thousand-dollars-a-year habits.

F.U.M.A.
F.U. MONEY ASSIGNMENTS

1. *What resources, what new knowledge do you need to acquire in order to make your F.U. Money?"*

2. *What new skills do you need to develop in order to make your F.U. Money?*

3. *Make a list of five habits that prevent you from making your F.U. Money. (HINT: procrastination, fear of taking risks, unwilling to invest in your education, too much TV, lack of focus, lack of discipline, lack of follow through.)*

    1. _____

    2. _____

    3. _____

    4. _____

    5. _____

Now, come up with at least two alternatives to replace each old habit.

OLD HABIT:
    Alternative 1. _____
    Alternative 2. _____

OLD HABIT:
    Alternative 1. _____
    Alternative 2. _____

OLD HABIT:
    Alternative 1. _____
    Alternative 2. _____

OLD HABIT:
    Alternative 1. _____
    Alternative 2. _____

OLD HABIT:
    Alternative 1. _____
    Alternative 2. _____

CHAPTER 9

F.U. MONEY MYTH #7: YOU HAVE TO WORK HARD TO MAKE MONEY

Do you know someone who works very hard and doesn't make a lot of money? If working hard is the path to F.U. Money, why isn't my nice garbage man a millionaire? You must realize that a good work ethic alone won't get you to the bank.

We are taught that the only way to make REAL money is by working hard, struggling, and enduring hardship after hardship.

Only at that point do you become "honored" in the world's eyes. Hence, that's where the term "hard-earned" dollars came from. It's like you're considered more worthy if you make the money in a difficult fashion. Why would you buy into that bullshit?

Just think: when you go to the bank and make a deposit, does the clerk ask you, "Sir or ma'am, how hard did you have to work to get this money?" or "I am sorry, we can't accept this deposit because you make this money without breaking a sweat." They just want to know how much. They don't give a shit how hard you had to work to get it.

Or let's say it's your birthday and you go buy yourself a sport car. The car salesperson doesn't care if that money "came too easy." When I buy my girlfriend a Louis Vuitton, I can assure you she has absolutely no idea where the money even comes from and she couldn't care less.

When you're able to afford the best college for your kids, your kids don't care if you worked yourself to death to make the money or if you made it "easy."

Let's take this a step further. I'll describe two men. Let's say both of them make good money. Who you think would have more potential for being a great husband and a great father?

Someone who works eighty to ninety hours a week, who's rarely home and even when he is home, is exhausted, unhealthy, and still preoccupied with work...

...OR a man who works only twenty or thirty hours a week, perhaps works from home, controls his own schedule, who has the time and is ABLE to prioritize his important relationships, takes care of his health, and isn't constantly preoccupied and worried about work?

I think the answer is obvious.

Now, this isn't to say that a hard-working man can't be a great husband and father. In fact, considering the circumstances, any man who pulls this off should be highly respected. And this isn't to say that a man who has more free time will automatically be a great husband and father. He could be a total asshole.

But looking at the above scenario, doesn't it seem that the man who makes EASY money has stacked the odds more in his favor, that he has the POTENTIAL of becoming a great husband and father?

Here's the bottom line: you don't get some kind of bonus if you work harder than someone else for the same amount of money. I am

NOT saying don't work hard. What I am saying is you have to work hard on the right things if you ever want to make your F.U. Money.

I'm trying to get you to think differently about the concept of money. Is this making sense to you? Making money doesn't have to be a struggle. Plus, you don't have to make it slowly. In fact, if you're going to work hard anyway, you might as well get rich… and the faster, the better.

OPEN AN EASY MONEY ACCOUNT TODAY

LOKISM #23

Don't just work hard, work hard at working smart.

I have two bank accounts. One is the hard-earned dollars account, the other one is the easy money account. All the money in the easy money account is money that I've created from residual income, no real work on my part, and little or no active labor.

When you are able to generate "easy money," there's no need to feel guilty when you spend it, is there?

One time, I bought my mom an ultra-luxury cruise on Mother's Day (she came from a poor family and had never been on a cruise before), she said, "Dan, I don't want you to spend your hard-earned dollars on me. I don't need this. You're wasting your money."

I just laughed and answered, "Don't worry, Mom. This money is from my easy money account. It didn't take me a lot of effort to get this money."

HOW DO YOU MAKE EASY MONEY?

Anytime you're swapping hours for dollars, you're not making easy money. It doesn't matter what you're doing, how much you enjoy it, or how much you're getting paid to do it.

Even if you're getting paid one thousand dollars an hour to be an ice cream tester at Ben & Jerry's, it's not MY definition of easy money. Although if they pay me, I might agree to do it for a day.

Easy money comes when you're leveraging other people's time, knowledge, and energy so you make money while you sleep. Easy money comes when you're using your intelligence, not doing manual labor to make money.

Easy money comes when your physical presence and your direct involvement aren't required to make the money.

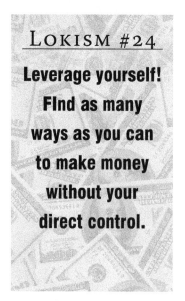

LOKISM #24

Leverage yourself! FInd as many ways as you can to make money without your direct control.

DOING THINGS ONCE AND GETTING PAID AGAIN AND AGAIN

There are all sorts of ways to build income by leveraging other people's efforts and skill sets. For instance, I have sold millions of dollars worth of products over the Internet using affiliates to market them for me. During this process alone, I've demonstrated the power of using numerous kinds of leverage:

1. I created the product once, yet I keep getting paid for it every time someone buys it. So I do the work once yet keep getting paid over and over. That's leverage.

2. I've created some products that are actually compilations of interviews with other people. This way, I don't even have to come up with the content myself. I'm simply leveraging the expertise of others to create a product that puts easy money into my pocket.

3. I have the graphic art, the website and the sales letter all created by someone else. That's leveraging other people's skill sets to get things done professionally and FAST.

4. I promote the product using an affiliate network. I pay the affiliates a commission only if they make a sale. This allows me to leverage the time, effort, and influence of literally thousands of website owners.

That's just one simple example of how you can do something once and get paid for years to come. It's all about leverage. Leverage as I define it is maximum productivity with minimum effort.

As John D. Rockefeller said, "I have ways of making money that you know nothing of." There are so many ways you can make the money you deserve without endless hours of work if you just take the time and effort to learn them. With all the information available today, you really have no excuse to stay in the same old rut.

LOKISM #25

Leverage is maximum productivity with minimum effort.

F.U.M.A.
F.U. MONEY ASSIGNMENTS

Brainstorm at least twenty ways you can generate more income without working harder. Go through them and highlight the ideas that resonate with you the most.

1. _____
2. _____
3. _____
4. _____
5. _____
6. _____
7. _____
8. _____
9. _____
10. _____
11. _____
12. _____
13. _____
14. _____
15. _____
16. _____
17. _____
18. _____
19. _____
20. _____

Who do you need to talk to in order to get these ideas into action?

CHAPTER 10

F.U. MONEY MYTH #8: YOU HAVE TO BE PERFECTLY READY

Have you ever heard of the saying, "Success is when preparation meets with opportunity"?

I've got news for you. No matter how much you prepare, you'll never be totally prepared for every opportunity. If you wait for perfect conditions before you seize an opportunity, you'll be waiting till the day you die.

I wasn't ready when I quit my job. I wasn't ready when I started a business. I wasn't ready when I put up my first website. I wasn't ready when I wrote my first book. I wasn't ready when I had to deliver a presentation in front of thousands of people. I wasn't ready when I made my first million. I probably wasn't ready for every major opportunity that presented itself in my life—but I was comfortable.

I like what Mark Burnett, the creator of *Survivor* and *The Apprentice* outlines as his philosophy of business in his book *Jump In!: Even If You Don't Know How to Swim*: "Nothing will ever be totally perfect, and nothing can be totally planned. The best you can hope for is to be about half certain of your plan and know that you and the team you've assembled are willing to work hard enough to overcome the inevitable problems as they arrive. And arrive they will."

Another thing that holds people back is that they say to themselves, "But I don't know how to do it." Well, here's my answer to that: you don't have to know how to do something before you do it!

LOKISM #26

Rich people make themselves do what they don't know how to do—until they do know how to do it.

Here's an example: let's say you're being forced to run a marathon a year from now. For argument's sake, let's say you're not allowed to read a book on running marathons, you're not allowed to buy special equipment, and you're not even allowed to get advice from another marathon runner. Yet you still have to be prepared, because a year from now you know you're going to run the marathon.

My question is, can you still prepare yourself to run the damn marathon? Absolutely! How? Put on your running shoes and start running! You can learn as you go.

People use fear of not knowing something as an excuse for not getting started. It's called "paralysis of analysis." You'll see this a lot on the seminar circuit. People go from one seminar to another, seeking all the "answers" before they get started. As a result, they never get started. They're hiding behind the education, scared to death of making a mistake.

Now, I'm not saying don't get an education. But don't get hung up on the details. You can figure it out as you go. Get off your ass and do something.

The answers always come as you're working on it.

DO YOU HAVE TO TEACH A CHILD TO WALK?

Think about it. You don't have to "teach" children to walk before they will start trying. They don't need to watch instructional DVD's or attend seminars. They don't stop to ask mom or dad, "Now, how do I do this?"

Nope. Someday they just decide they're tired of crawling and they're ready to walk. They pull themselves up on the nearest sturdy object and go for it.

They'll bump into furniture, fall on their butts, and sometimes end up with bruises, cuts, and scrapes in the process. They don't care. Why? Because they want to walk, dammit!

All of us start our lives this way—yet something happens as we grow older. I'm not sure what it is. Maybe it's the educational system that puts us in classrooms for twelve-plus years before we ever experience "real" life. We think we have to get educated thoroughly before we ever actually "do" something.

It didn't used to be this way. For thousands of years, trades were passed on from men to boys in the form of apprenticeships.

Boys had "masters" until they were twenty-one years old, and the masters taught them how to do a particular trade—not in a "classroom" environment but in a work environment. In other words, the apprentices learned by doing, not just by "listening."

SCHOOL IS NEVER OUT FOR THE PRO

I'm not knocking education. In fact, school is NEVER out for the pros. There is no "graduation." You never actually "graduate" because you never stop learning.

You have to stay on top of your game—always. I have a library of over a thousand books. I strive to stay on top, so I read books and listen to others who I know who—most importantly—are qualified to speak.

When people ask me, "Do you have an MBA?" I always reply, "I do, but not the kind of MBA that most people have. I have a different kind of MBA—Massive Bank Account."

LOKISM #27

Business is the ultimate school of learning.

That's my qualification. I graduated from the school of hard knocks. The best stuff I've learned has been from my own experience, which has taught me things you can't learn in school—the same things I'm teaching you in this book.

I doubt you'll ever find a copy of F.U. Money in a school library. I've always wondered why they don't teach this stuff in school. I guess I'll never know.

DON'T WAIT UNTIL EVERYTHING IS JUST RIGHT BECAUSE IT WILL NEVER BE PERFECT

The DVD *The Secret®*, along with its corresponding book, was a bonafide self-help phenomenon.

Shortly after it was released in 2006, everybody from Oprah to Larry King was talking about it. From a marketing perspective, I thought it was brilliant. It's even semi-entertaining to watch.

It's basically a bunch of motivational and spiritual gurus talking into a camera, discussing how the "law of attraction" will somehow magically attract prosperity into your life. There they sit, trying to pull the wool over everybody's eyes that the secret to getting rich is that by thinking positively enough that the universe will somehow make you rich.

It's like saying if I wanted to lose weight, all I have to do is sit at home and visualize myself as slim and fit. And if I visualize hard enough, voila, I'll lose weight. Horseshit.

Now, am I saying that you don't need a positive mental attitude? No. In fact, you MUST start with a positive mental attitude if you ever want to succeed—but that's just the beginning.

It's not just about having the right attitude. There are so many other factors. It's not just having about the right attitude—you must combine it with the right abilities.

People would rather hear warm and fuzzy nonsense. It's a big, fat lie.

I was at a real estate seminar, and sitting in the audience next to me was a guy telling me, "I've been to ten different real estate seminars. I've learned how to buy real estate with nothing down... how to do lease options... how to negotiate... how to find motivated sellers... all that stuff. I've been following these speakers and trainers for a long time."

I said, "Great, so how many properties have you bought?"

Dead silence.

I asked again, "So how many properties have you bought?"

"None," he replied sheepishly.

LOKISM #28

Ready–fire–fire–fire–aim a little and then FIRE some more!

You see, people read books and go to seminars and expect to have all the answers and get all their ducks in a row before they take any action. They're afraid of making a mistake. They're afraid of getting started.

But guess what? You LEARN by making mistakes. In fact, it's fantastic to make mistakes! That means you're making progress. That means you're trying something new. You don't have to know something before you do it. Knowledge alone is NOT power. Knowledge is really only power in reserve. It's completely useless if it's not tapped into by applying action. Only applied knowledge is power.

We've all had it happen to us. We're watching TV or browsing through the airline catalog, and then we say to ourselves, "Hey! They stole my idea!" or better yet, "I thought of that ten years ago!"

Guess what? Others are profiting from your ideas because you were too damn lazy to act on them.

Without action, you could have the greatest idea and the greatest plan in the world and you would still fail. Whereas a modest idea and an incomplete plan often produce success when accompanied by enough action.

LOKISM #29

Ideas aren't worth shit unless acted upon.

Take massive, CONSTANT action. So you get a few bruises? So you make some mistakes, so fucking what? Get busy failing. Remember, you don't have to get it right, you just have to get it going.

F.U.M.A.
F.U. MONEY ASSIGNMENTS

Finish the following sentence five times.

If I knew I couldn't fail, I would…

1. _____

2. _____

3. _____

4. _____

5. _____

Finish the following sentence five times.

If I had all the skills, intelligence, and contacts I need right now to make my F.U. Money, I would…

1. _____

2. _____

3. _____

4. _____

5. _____

part 3:
THE F.U.
MONEY
MINDSET

CHAPTER 11

WHY F.U. MONEY IS NOT FOR THE TOUCHY-FEELY

Can everyone make F.U. Money? Hell no. In fact, it's for a very small percentage of the population. These are people who think and act different than everyone else.

Not everyone is meant to be or even wants to make F.U. Money. If it's not you, that's okay. Some people just don't have it in them. It doesn't make you a bad person. If that's you, don't beat yourself up.

Be whatever you want to be. If you're satisfied with having just enough money to get by, buying only what you need to be moderately happy, or simply get through to the next paycheck. That's fine with me.

However, if you WANT to make your F.U. Money—if you WANT to be financially free for the rest of your life—you MUST be committed. You can't just stick your toe in the water. It's a total commitment.

None of this bullshit like saying one week, "I'm going to make my F.U. Money" and the next week, "Nah. This is too damn hard."

You're either in or you're out. You have to keep the commitment day-in and day-out, every single day until they put you six feet under. There's no testing the water in this deal.

LOKISM #30

The secret to wealth is committing to ONE idea over time.

You have to make F.U. Money the number one priority in your life to get there as quickly as humanly possible.

Most people just don't have that kind of commitment. They are not inclined to be wealthy in the first place, and they don't have the wherewithal inside them to get there if they did.

If you look around you, this is obvious. It's why 95 percent of the population is broke or living paycheck to paycheck and sadly, it will ALWAYS be that way.

THE WORLD IS FULL OF CRAP

Nobody wants you to succeed.

They might tell you that they do, but don't believe them—it's just lip service. Your relatives might say so, or even your friends, but they're lying to your face.

Do you honestly believe they want you to grow into a F.U. Money Millionaire while they're down in the gutter, sucking paychecks? I don't think so.

Think about it. When you told your friends and family that you were gonna quit your job and start your own business, what did they say to you? Were they supportive? I doubt it.

So don't believe a word of the crap they tell you. People want to see you fail so they can have someone to blame and justify their own failures. "Oh, look at John and Mary, they couldn't make it. Well, I told them they shouldn't have started their own business in the first place. If they had just listened to me, he would still have his good, secure job... blah, blah, blah."

Bullshit!

If you're going to make your F.U. Money, you have to plow through mounds of crap from all sides.

You will have to fight and push through a world of lies, unsupportive mindsets, struggles, and hardships to move closer to your goal every single day. You're going to have to FIGHT for uninterrupted time so you can focus on your goals with laser-like intensity.

In the process, you'll piss some people off. Friends will think you're "dissing" them. Family members will think you're a workaholic. They'll accuse you of misplacing your "priorities"—of being obsessed, money-hungry, or just plain greedy.

To add insult to injury, if you have any feelings of self-doubt, add those to the shit that others are feeding you and it makes it tough as hell.

Plus, to round it all off, the chance of you actually making it and living your dream is LOW. Now how's that for motivation?

So do you want it? Do you REALLY want it? I hope so. If you are ready to do whatever the hell it takes—as long as it's moral, ethical, and legal—then keep reading.

WHO ARE YOU LISTENING TO?

The world has an opinion and it's usually worth exactly what it costs: nothing. It's worthless.

People are like crabs in a bucket. If you put a bunch of crabs in a bucket, you don't have to put a lid on the bucket to keep them from escaping. Because if a crab starts climbing up, the ones on the bottom will ALWAYS pull the climbing ones down to their level.

The world doesn't want you to win. The vast majority of people will NEVER make their F.U. Money, nor will they ever try. They want you to be down in the gutter with them so they have somebody else whose shoulder they can cry on.

Is your friend rich? Is your brother-in-law rich? When they give you advice, should you listen? Yes. Go ahead—be polite. Then you can toss their advice right out the window as soon as they walk out of the room.

It never ceases to amaze me how people will suck up any information, take it to heart, and make decisions based on the hot air that comes out of other people's mouths!

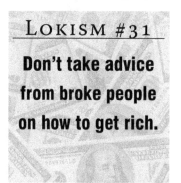

LOKISM #31

Don't take advice from broke people on how to get rich.

The sad part is that sometimes even when you pay for service, you can't trust it. Have you ever gotten bad advice from an attorney? I know I have!

Even if you take advice from a professional, you still have to determine if that advice is applicable to you (that includes taking advice from me, by the way). The final decision still falls on your shoulders. You have the final say.

So be very careful to whom you listen. If you want to be a F.U. Money Millionaire, you'd better learn from one.

IT DOESN'T MATTER WHAT THE MORONS SAY

From the time that you were born until now, you have been conditioned to be broke.

Virtually everyone you've come into contact with your entire life has been conditioned to be broke. Therefore, by surrounding yourselves with these people, you have been conditioned to be broke, too.

If you're like most people, unless you're born with a silver spoon in your mouth:

- the minute you are born the first person that touched you after you were delivered was a nurse… and he/she was broke (and hell, in this day and age, the doctor was probably broke, too).
- and then (unless your last name is Hilton or Trump) you were handed to your broke parents…
- who then put you into a grade school taught by broke teachers…
- then you went to high school and were taught by more broke teachers…
- then you may have gone to college and you were taught by broke professors…
- then you graduated and got a job working for broke managers…
- all so you could then hang out with friends and relatives that are also broke.

Now, can you see how you have been conditioned to be broke? Think about this.

ARE ALL YOUR FRIENDS BROKE?

Take it one step further and ask yourself, "How many rich people do I even know personally?"

Sure, you may be acquainted with a few, but do you really know them? Are you friends with them, or better yet, are you involved in business with them or do you enjoy a mentoring or mastermind relationship with them?

For most people, if they do know someone who is wealthy, it's some person they've played tennis or golf with, who attends their church, or whom they've worked for in some capacity. The wealthy person knows who they are and maybe considers them a friend, but that's where the relationship ends.

Ask yourself, "Are the relationships I have with the wealthy people in my life going to positively impact my finances anytime soon?

I'm not saying that you need to try to "use" wealthy people or see them as a means to an end. As we've seen already, you've been conditioned to be broke by broke people your whole life—due to no choice of your own.

LOKISM #32

Do the opposite of what everyone else does and you will almost always succeed.

To recondition yourself for wealth instead, you need more than wealthy friends. You need to cultivate relationships with wealthy friends or business associates that will positively impact your MIND and, therefore, your future.

YOU HAVE TO BE A LITTLE "WEIRD" TO MAKE YOUR F.U. MONEY

Just the fact that you're reading this book means you have to be a little on the "weird" side. Why? Because according to the American Booksellers Association:

- 80% of Americans did not buy or read a book this year
- 70% of American adults have NOT been in a bookstore in the last five years
- 58% of American adults have never read a book after high school

As you can see, just by getting this far you're in the minority! In fact, I've had people call me crazy, insane, and outrageous in my business career just because I've taken a few risks and endured a few failures.

Yet even when I show them that I've made it through the challenges and I now have the money to back up my big mouth, people have the nerve to call me eccentric.

It doesn't make any sense. Most people go through their lives dirt broke and working for someone else until they die—and they call me eccentric? Why? Because I have the balls to step out on my own, apply what I've PAID to learn, and as a result, achieve staggering wealth? I'm the eccentric one? Are you fucking kidding me?

If you want to follow in my footsteps, you'll have to get used to this kind of reaction from people. F.U. Money is not for everyone. It's not "normal." You don't do "normal" things to achieve wealth. In fact, if you do things "normal," you'll be broke, like every other "normal" person.

F.U.M.A.
F.U. MONEY ASSIGNMENTS

Who are the people you admire because they're successful at what they do? What qualities and skills do they have?

_____

How many of those qualities and skills do you have, too? Which ones can you develop?

_____

CHAPTER 12

IF YOUR LIFE STINKS, IT'S YOUR OWN DAMN FAULT

A few months ago I was on a call with a coaching client named Ron. He said, "Dan, I need some help. My business isn't doing well, my competitors are furious, and all my customers are cheapskates. And my vendors want to jack up their prices and the economy is really bad now."

"C'mon Ron! You're just bitching and moaning here," I replied.

"Dan, but you don't understand, my business sucks."

"You know what, Ron? I've got a solution for you. Let me help you out with that."

"Please, please tell me. What's the answer?"

"It's very simple, Ron, if your business sucks, it's because as a businessperson, you SUCK."

Dead silence.

"But, Dan, I—"

I interrupted, "Ron, listen: every business is a reflection of its owner. Let me ask you a question: are there other businesses in your industry that are kicking your ass?"

"Well, yes."

"Their business is booming, and yet they are essentially selling very similar products as you, is that correct?"

"Uh-hum, yeah. I guess that's true."

"If that's the case, it means there's something YOU don't know—so it's incompetence on YOUR part. And until you realize you ARE the problem—that YOU are the cause of the struggle—you can't fix it. Do you see where I'm coming from?"

"I got it, Dan."

LOKISM #33

Every business is a reflection of its owner.

F.U. Money begins when you take full 100 percent responsibility for your life. Stop blaming the government, the politicians, lawyers (okay, maybe you CAN blame lawyers a little bit), bad luck, your parents, your employees, the economy, and the weather, etc.

The buck always stops with YOU.

FAST FOOD IS MAKING YOU FAT?

You see, most people paint themselves as victims of circumstance. Don't believe me? Just watch an episode of Jerry Springer.

The entire fucking show is based on victims—how somebody did somebody wrong, had sex with somebody else, whatever—and then the hilarity ensues when all the drama, crying, fighting, and hitting each other kicks into full gear. Somebody else is always the cause of all the victim's problems. It's pathetic.

If you want to get rich, you can't be a victim. Our society is full of victims. Like the guy who eats fast food every day for years and then sues the fast food restaurants for making him fat.

Tell me this: who chose to get up every morning, every day, and drive to the restaurant? Who looked at the menu, placed an order, pulled out his wallet, and bought the food? Who chose to shovel the large fries, double cheeseburger, and a milkshake down his throat? Exactly. The guy. The customer. The "victim."

IF YOU CAN'T FIND GOOD PEOPLE TO HELP YOU, MAYBE YOU'RE NOT A GOOD PERSON

Entrepreneurs say to me all the time, "Dan, I can't get good help these days." I always reply, "Maybe that's because you're a lousy leader! The problem is NOT that you can't find good people. The real problem is GOOD people don't WANT to come work for you. Why? Maybe you can't afford to pay the salaries that really good people deserve."

"But, Dan, my business is not doing well. I can't afford to pay them that much money." Again, I'm not sympathetic. "That's because you're a lousy business owner! Your profit is low, your revenue is low, and now you can't afford to have a team. Heck, you don't even know how to build a team."

If this is the case for you, then you have to take responsibility. That's a tough pill to swallow, I know—because I've had to swallow it myself a few times!

I even find myself being in the victim mode from time to time. When that happens, I stop and ask myself, "Am I acting like a victim or am I acting like an owner?" And I find that when I take 100 percent responsibility for my life, something magical happens.

Lokism #34

**There are three kinds of people:
1) People who wait for things to happen
2) People who make things happen
3) People who wonder what the fuck just happened.**

WHAT YOU WOULD AND WOULD NOT DO FOR MONEY

Have you ever watched the TV show *Fear Factor*? The whole show is based simply on watching what some people would or would NOT do for money.

It's fascinating to watch the dangerous stunts people will do and the risks they will take. It's downright disturbing to see some of the gross stuff that they're willing to eat: smelly rotten entrails of dead animals, creepy crawly insects, you name it, just for the chance at winning a measly fifty thousand bucks!

Sure, *Fear Factor* is an extreme example. But it IS important for you to be clear and to know up front what you would and would NOT do for money, because when you do, it's incredibly liberating.

Now, let me clarify: I'm NOT talking about deciding whether or not you would do something illegal, immoral, or crazy to make money. That's not what I mean at all.

HOW BAD DO YOU WANT IT?

That's an important question that you should ask yourself about what price you WOULD be willing to pay to make your F.U. Money. Here are some examples:

- Say you've decided that you want to get rich in real estate. Great. Now ask yourself if you really know HOW to get rich in real estate.

  If not, how are you going to learn? Are you willing to attend seminars, read books, and/or join a coaching program, etc., to learn how to get rich in real estate?

  If you said yes, how much are you willing to spend for your education? Five thousand dollars? Ten thousand? Twenty thousand? Do you know?

  In other words, what are you willing to do and what are you NOT willing to do to make money?

- Say you want to make a fortune on the Internet. Okay. Here's the thing: I can say from experience that building a business from scratch online, even if you KNOW what you're doing (and most people don't), takes money and time. In fact, the LESS money you have, the more TIME you have to invest in your Internet venture. There's no way around it.

  So ask yourself, if you have a regular day job but don't have a lot of money, are you willing to spend your free time on evenings and weekends doing the "free" things online that will drive traffic to your site? How LONG are you willing to keep doing these things without turning a profit? A month? Six months? A year?

  Or, if you don't have a lot of time but you do have some money to spend, how much money are you willing to spend to send PAID traffic to your Web site? How much money are you willing to LOSE while you're learning how this game is played? *Do you know?*

Figure out what you ARE willing to do and what are you NOT willing to do to make money.

"You must determine the price that you will have to pay to achieve success, and then get busy paying that price."
- H.L. HUNT (TEXAS OIL TYCOON)

CHAPTER 13

YOU CAN'T HAVE THE GLORY IF YOU DON'T HAVE THE GUTS

My good friend, Peter Sage, suffered from a major financial setback a few years ago. He decided to walk away from a big investment deal due to ethical reasons, and the decision had a significant impact on this net worth. He was a very successful entrepreneur, yet he found himself basically starting again from scratch.

At the time, Peter was living in the UK and he made a decision to move to Vancouver to begin a new chapter of his life. While he was hoping to move to Vancouver in about two or three months, he sat on the beach in Sydney and asked himself, "If I could wave a magic wand and sprinkle some fairy dust on my business to get back on my feet, what would I need to do?"

Again, this goes back to knowing exactly what you want—gaining clarity in your vision. He wanted to buy his dream penthouse in

Vancouver. It was a HUGE goal, especially for where he was at the time financially.

Peter jumped on the Internet at night just to look for new pictures. He believes in having pictures of what you want on a "goal map" to remind him on a daily basis to get in touch with his inspiration. It motivates him. It helps him to focus.

Through the search engines he found the most gorgeous apartment he had ever seen. He said, "WOW. That's it!" It was one of those love-at-first-sight feelings. No questions. No further discussions. This was the one! It was amazing.

It was exactly the place he had dreamed of living. It was the price he'd written down. It was THE ONE.

There was just one problem. It cost four million dollars. It was way out of his league, especially since he'd just lost a lot of money from the investment deal.

But he had a dream, and he was committed. He thought to himself, "Maybe if I string the seller and realtor along for six months, get a lawyer to put in an offer, I'll get close."

The penthouse was his focus! He became obsessed. No ifs, no maybes, no let me think about it. It was about midnight in the UK and it was four p.m. Canadian time when he rang the number for the real estate agent.

"Hi, this is Peter Sage. I was searching the Internet and I stumbled across your listing. I'm sort of interested in this apartment." (He was trying to sound casual)

The agent replied, "You called at the perfect time. A sale just fell through two days ago."

Peter believed it was meant to be. The apartment had his name on it. He just had to have it. It turned out he was in a contract race with quite a few interested buyers and he needed to put down a 10 percent deposit in twenty-four hours. Again, WAY of his league.

Plus, because he wasn't a Canadian resident, he was required to get a non-status mortgage, which meant he had to come up another 25 percent down on top of the 10 percent in a few months. If he didn't, under Canadian law, he'd lose the 10 percent. It was a nonrefundable deposit!

So it was a total of 35 percent deposit, with four hundred thousand dollars to lose if he didn't cough up another one million in a few months!

You want to talk about commitment? THAT'S commitment. He made a decision to buy his dream apartment when he had no idea how the hell he was going to come up with the money.

Later, Peter told me he made the jump based on ONE simple principle of goal setting:

Where's the room for inspiration, creativity, and growth? NONE!

Within twenty-four hours, Peter managed to refinance his house; he maxed out ALL his credit cards; he borrowed some money here, there, and everywhere; and he wired across the 10 percent and signed the nonrefundable deposit.

LOKISM #35

If you set a goal NOW and you see a path of how you're gonna achieve it, by definition, the goal is too small.

Now he had a much bigger mountain to climb. He had to come up with a million dollars within a period of weeks. Otherwise, he'd lose everything. How crazy was that?

FORTUNE FAVORS THE BOLD

Peter burned all his ships. He had no way out. There was no "if," no "maybe," no "I'll try"—it was DO or DIE.

Peter was going to make it happen no matter what! He was gonna do whatever the hell it took! He HAD to find a way. That level of commitment is what creates results.

Within weeks, he tied up acres of land with an option. He divided them up and sold them to multiple buyers, and he made more than enough profits to come up with the additional 25 percent down payment for his apartment.

In fact, I was just at his place. It's spectacular, absolutely breathtaking.

Was it stupid? Wasn't it risky? Was he nuts? Or was he simply committed and passionate about his dream?

If Peter had been anything other than red-hot he would have lost his ass on the deal. Lukewarm would never have worked. That's guts. I respect and admire people who've got guts! I am proud to have a friend like him.

Are you willing to give up your "security" in exchange of financial freedom? What are you willing to sacrifice to make your F.U. Money?

A PAY PRICE TO ACTION

I was in my local bookstore and bumped into one of my college buddies. He almost didn't recognize me, but I recognized him.

He asked, "How the hell have you been, man? You look good."

"Thank you."

"Dan, what have you been up to?"

I said, "Nothing much. Just busy growing my businesses."

We chatted briefly. I found out he was working in a local restaurant as a waiter. I didn't tell him what I was up to because he would never understand, and frankly I didn't feel like explaining it.

I can still clearly remember that he was always into sports. He was on the basketball team, the stud that got all the girls—one of the coolest guys on campus. Everybody wanted to hang out with him.

On the other hand, I was the geek who sat in the very back of the room, afraid to put up my hand and ask questions. I was the quiet one who was shy and didn't make eye contact with people when I talked to them. I would just go home and not participate in any after-class activities because of the language barrier. People didn't even remember my name. I was invisible.

But while all of the cool guys were going to parties, chasing girls, getting drunk, and having fun, I would lock myself in a room and read business books like a madman.

I had started my copyrighting career at the age of nineteen, so I was studying sales letters and writing copy for clients. They all thought I was the geek, the weirdo. You see, success takes discipline—so much so that your friends might start calling you Yoda!

> *"You can lose a lot of money chasing women, but*
> *you will never lose women chasing money."*
> **-Movie *I Think I Love My Wife***

I chose to forego a little immediate recreation, reward, and pleasure for future security. Everything in life comes with an opportunity cost. When you choose to do one thing, you automatically choose NOT to do other things. You have to give up something to get something.

The price for F.U. Money is self-discipline and self-control. Even when I was nineteen, I knew where I was headed. I knew even then what I wanted to do in life. If it meant I had to sacrifice a little fun, that's a price I gladly paid. And I'm damn glad that I figured it out as early as I did.

You gotta do what you gotta do.

I made some sacrifices early on, but looking back I have no regrets. I'm damn glad that I decided early on to do what I did. When I think back on all that nonsense that my college buddies were up to, and I compare it to the lifestyle I have now, there's no fucking way I would trade it for the world.

Success doesn't happen by accident. I chose to be successful. I chose to be happy. I chose to make my F.U. Money, and I chose to be fulfilled. I chose to give up a few fun time, and look at my life today.

LOKISM #36

The rich do what is hard; that's why their life is easy. Poor people do what's easy; that's why their life is hard.

I've made my F.U. Money. I have enough to live comfortably for the rest of my life. I can do what I want, when I want, with no worries.

I don't need a job. I can live life entirely on my own terms.

I did what was hard. I did what other people were not willing to do. I gladly paid the price that other people were not willing to pay. I endured the pain, hassle, and pressure that nobody else was willing to bear. That's why I now have the easy life that most people can only dream of.

HOW BAD DO YOU WANT IT?

If you're not where you want to be financially today, let me ask you just how bad you want it. What price are you willing to pay to get what you want?

You deserve nothing. You must earn everything. If you really want to make your F.U. Money, you must decide what you are going to DO today that will move you closer to your goal—and then get busy doing it. Not tomorrow—TODAY.

Yes, there's a price to pay to get there, and it will require some initial work plus a willingness to learn and grow on your part. But once you arrive, you will gladly say you'd do it all over again.

If you'd like to leave the cubicle life behind and fire your boss, go to www.fumoney.com. You'll find additional tools and resources to help you make your F.U. Money quicker and easier.

CHAPTER 14

WHY CONVENTIONAL WISDOM IS ALMOST ALWAYS WRONG

Conventional wisdom is the scripture of mediocrity. Mediocre beliefs create mediocre results. Conventional wisdom is for the masses. Are the masses broke or rich? Exactly.

"Cut up your credit cards, live below your means, and invest in a long-term well-diversified mutual fund."

"High expectations can lead to high levels of disappointment."

"You can't have your cake and eat it, too."

"A good job is the way to become rich."

"You better save your pennies for a rainy day."

"To get rich, you have to be a crook, a liar, a thief, or get lucky."

FUCK THAT.

I still remember my mom saying to me when I was a little kid, "Clean your plate, Dan, there are children starving in China."

I would ask, "But, Mom, how is cleaning my plate gonna help the starving children in China?" I never got an answer.

She would also say stuff like: Close the fridge, you're letting the air out; money doesn't grow on trees; and when I was young all I got was a pair of socks for my birthday, and I was happy to get them.

Did you hear that kind of stuff growing up? All of us got this kind of "scarcity thinking" pounded into us. Why? Because our parents got it pounded into them by their parents!

Here's another good one: "If God wanted us to have money he would give it to us." About that, I say the Lord helps those who help themselves.

It reminds me of the story from the movie *The Pursuit of Happyness* with Will Smith:

> *There was a man who was drowning, and a boat came, and the man on the boat said, "Do you need help?" and the man said, "God will save me." Then another boat came and tried to help him, but he said, "God will save me." Then he drowned and went to Heaven. Then the man asked God, "God, why didn't you save me?" and God said, "I sent you two boats, you dummy!"*

So do you have a plan, or do you expect the Lord to provide?

Here's a series of quotes that reinforces the idea that conventional wisdom is almost always wrong:

"We don't like their sound, and guitar music is on the way out."
-DECCA RECORDING CO., REJECTING THE BEATLES, 1962

"This 'telephone' has too many shortcomings to be seriously considered as a means of communication."
-WESTERN UNION INTERNAL MEMO, 1876

"There is no reason anyone would want a computer in their home."
-KEN OLSON, PRESIDENT, CHAIRMAN, AND FOUNDER
OF DIGITAL EQUIPMENT CORP., 1977

*"The concept is interesting and well-formed, but in order
to earn better than a 'C,' the idea must be feasible."*
-A YALE UNIVERSITY MANAGEMENT PROFESSOR IN RESPONSE TO
FRED SMITH'S PAPER PROPOSING RELIABLE OVERNIGHT DELIVERY
SERVICE (SMITH WENT ON TO FOUND FEDERAL EXPRESS)

"Everything that can be invented has been invented."
- CHARLES H. DUELL, COMMISSIONER,
U.S. OFFICE OF PATENTS, 1899

*"If I had thought about it. I wouldn't have done the experiment.
The literature was full of examples that said you can't do this."*
- SPENCER SILVER ON THE WORK THAT LED TO THE
UNIQUE ADHESIVES FOR 3-M "POST-IT" NOTES

CONVENTIONAL WISDOM HAS BEEN HOLDING PEOPLE BACK FOR CENTURIES

All of our lives, we are told by our peers that our goals are not realistic. Our dreams are too far-fetched. Our expectations are too high.

We're told, "You have to remember who you are and where you came from."

What? Who the hell gives a shit where I came from? All I need to know is where I'm going!

They preach to us that "those things" are for "other" people; we certainly can't expect that for ourselves; who are we kidding? Who do we think we are?

It reminds me of another story.

A young newlywed was preparing a ham for Christmas dinner. She carefully cut off the end of the ham before placing it in the pan for roasting.

Her husband asked her, "Why did you cut off the end of the ham?" And she replied, "I really don't know. My mother always did, so I thought you were supposed to."

Later, when talking to her mother, she asked her why she cut off the end of the ham before roasting it, and her mother replied, "I really don't know, but that's the way my mom always did it."

A few weeks later while visiting her grandmother, the young woman asked, "Grandma, why is it that you cut off the end of a ham before you roast it?"

Her grandmother replied, "Well, dear, it would never fit into my roasting pan."

You see, all of their lives people do what they're *familiar with*. They think that, since it's conventional wisdom, "Oh well, that's the way we've been doing it for years" although it's as plain as the nose on their face that it doesn't work. Yet you're supposed to keep doing it that way instead of thinking for yourself.

THE SUPER RICH ALWAYS GO AGAINST CONVENTIONAL WISDOM

You see, all super-successful people—wealthy people—go against conventional wisdom, like Ted Turner, Lee Iacocca, Henry Ford, Michael Dell, Thomas Edison, Bill Gates, Steve Jobs, and Fred Smith.

Probably any super-successful people you know all subscribed to doing what others felt was wrong.

Colonel Sanders was sixty-five years old when he decided to sell fried chicken in a cardboard box. He founded KFC. Richard Branson has spent his entire career having people tell him he was doing things the wrong way. He broke every bit of conventional business wisdom there is. And he's a fucking billionaire, for God's sake.

"DAN, YOU CAN'T DO THAT"

All my life I've had people tell me, "Dan, you can't do that." But I did it anyway—and I'm glad I did because I wouldn't be where I am today if I'd listened.

Now, below is a list of things that people told me that I couldn't do, but I did anyway:

1. You can't immigrate to a foreign country where you don't speak the language!
2. You can't go to college!
3. You can't drop out of college and still be a success!
4. You can't start your own business! You don't have a business degree.
5. You can't live an outrageous life and ever amount to anything!
6. You can't become a professional copywriter. You flunked English when you were in high school!
7. You can't become one of the highest paid copywriters in two years!
8. You can't charge one thousand dollars an hour for consulting!
9. You can't fire your clients!
10. You can't be a public speaker; it's your number one fear!
11. You can't write a sales letter that generates a million dollars in sales!

12. You can't write another sales letter that generates TWO million dollars in sales!

13. You can't get a five-hundred-million-dollar man to be your mentor!

14. You can't get a billionaire to be your mentor!

15. You can't make money on the Internet!

16. You can't publish a book!

17. You can't become a best-selling author!

18. You can't lose a quarter of a million dollars and come back!

19. You can't be the number one expert in your field!

20. You can't invest in real estate!

21. You can't just work four days a week.

22. You can't be a millionaire doing what you love!

23. You can't be a multimillionaire and live life entirely on your own terms!

24. You can't have it ALL!

There are probably a LOT more. I just came up with this list off the top of my head!

Bottom line: I HATE conventional wisdom.

So next time, when someone says to you, "You can't do that!" You had better reply, "Yeah? Watch me!"

CHAPTER 15

THE MOST IMPORTANT THING YOU CAN DO TODAY
TO START YOURSELF ON THE PATH TO F.U. MONEY

Contrary to conventional wisdom, again, self-love is very good. It's healthy. Think about it: if you don't love yourself, how can you expect anybody else to love you? You can't!

Let me ask you a question. Think about the successful people that you admire. Just pick any one person or group of successful people that you want to model and be where they are financially.

Ask yourself, "Do they have high self-esteem or low self-esteem?"

They have high esteem without exception. I have never met a super-successful person with low self-esteem. Why? Because self-esteem is the foundation of all success.

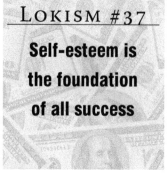

LOKISM #37

Self-esteem is the foundation of all success

DEVELOP A CAREFULLY-MEASURED ARROGANCE

I know this is a controversial, politically incorrect thing to say, but it's the truth. It's a very important lesson I learned from a billionaire: you need to develop a sense of superiority.

In order to make your F.U. Money, you must believe that you actually deserve all the success, wealth, and power that you seek.

It's not about being egotistical; it's about having certainty and confidence. In fact, it's IMPOSSIBLE to make your F.U. Money without it.

Most people never make their F.U. Money because of their low self-esteem. They're unsure about themselves, and it shows. They second-guess themselves and never get started as a result.

Here's the funny thing about all of this: it's okay to be unsure about what you're doing, but it's the kiss of DEATH not to be confident in yourself. If you aren't confident in yourself, you'll never DO anything in the first place! People who wait to be totally sure about what they're doing rarely ever get started.

COULD HAVE AND SHOULD HAVE

I'll prove it. Just go to a party and bring up the fact that you own your own business, or that you're thinking about starting one. Watch what happens.

You'll have tons of people listening who will chime in and say something like, "You know, I wish I could do that. I've always thought about breaking away and doing my own thing." They'll usually go into detail about some idea they've "always had" but never had the balls to pursue.

Bottom line: the vast majority of these people will NEVER do anything other than work for someone else. And yet they'll always bring up the same old bullshit line about "starting their own business" when someone brings it up!

The most successful entrepreneurs I know got that way because they had enough confidence in themselves to know that even if they didn't know exactly what they were doing when they started, they would figure things out as they went along. That's the difference. It's ALL about self-confidence.

Successful people are fully aware that they will encounter problems along the way, but it's their self-confidence that allows them to say, "That's okay—I'll be able to handle the problems as they come."

Your self-esteem is low because you haven't had any serious success in your life to make it high. Do you know the best thing to make low self-esteem disappear? It's called CASH—lots of it!

Warm and fuzzy motivational gurus tell you if you feel good about yourself, you'll get rich. I say if you make a ton of

LOKISM #38

Nothing great was ever achieved by timid people.

money, then you'll feel pretty damn good about yourself. As you make more money, the higher your self-esteem will become.

Before you know it, you'll become more powerful and decisive. Success breeds success. You'll look in the mirror, and you'll LOVE the NEW YOU. You'll admire yourself.

NOBODY LOVES DAN LOK MORE THAN DAN LOK

I love myself. If that sounds like I have a BIG ego, you're damn right I do. It comes from the control that I have over my life. It comes from my work ethic. It comes from knowing that I've done more preparation than the other guys.

To have self-confidence is to feel capable, sure of your abilities. Lack of confidence is fear that you lack the ability to do something. I've read over a thousand books when most people don't even read one book a year. I take risks and do things that people are not willing to do. That's what gives me the confidence. That's what gives me a sense of superiority—and there's not a damn thing wrong with it.

I'm the only child in my family. I came to North America when I couldn't speak a word of English; I felt like an outsider. I learned how to rely on myself. Am I self-centered? You bet I am, because I had to be.

My parents are divorced, and I've learned fast that nobody's going to come rescue me. Nobody else is going to make me successful. It's all about me. I want to make myself happy, not anybody else.

I decide things for myself and am willing to take all the criticism, all the blame—but also all the rewards. My success is not dependent on anyone or anything except me. That's exactly why I place a high value on myself, even if it means sometimes giving the appearance of arrogance to others. It's also why I don't care what other people think.

I was giving a seminar and a guy asked me, "Dan, it seems like you're full of yourself. Do you think you're the center of the universe?"

I responded, "Yes, I do think I am the center of the universe. Everything evolves around me. And I like it that way."

LOKISM #39

You can care about other people without caring what they think.

Now, this man was being a smartass, and certainly wasn't asking for my advice. In a way, my response was the BEST advice I could have given him. Why? Because my sense of superiority comes from confidence. And confidence comes from competence. If you know you can do something well, you're confident about it.

It comes from (and here's the key) knowing that I have the ability to make things happen. If this guy had taken his head out of his ass for a moment, he would have realized...

WHY LACKING SELF-CONFIDENCE IS INCREDIBLY SELFISH

If more people had this type of confidence, the world would be a better place. Think about it. The world will never know how many undiscovered "geniuses" there are—because of their lack of self-confidence. They will never reach their true potential.

Who knows, there's probably some person out there who has the ability to cure cancer. But if he doesn't have the self-confidence to step up to the plate, the world will never benefit from that knowledge.

Millions of people may continue to die needlessly because this person doesn't want to be so "arrogant" as to say to the world, "I can develop a cure for cancer," and take the steps necessary—regardless of the cost or the potential of numerous failed attempts.

Instead, he will sit in some office cubicle somewhere, wasting away, drawing a "comfortable" paycheck for the rest of his life. He will go to his grave without making the impact on the world that he COULD have—if only he had the guts.

LOKISM #40

Confidence comes from competence.

WHAT IF BILL GATES HAD STAYED AT HARVARD?

Bill Gates dropped out of Harvard because he saw the tremendous opportunity brewing in the software market. At the time, people thought he was nuts. Drop out of one of the most prestigious colleges in the world to pursue something "unproven"? Are you insane?

And yet, because Gates had the certainty and the confidence that he was doing the right thing, the world is a better place because of it.

If he had NOT taken action—if he had taken the "safe" route and just chucked the idea and finished his degree at Harvard—Microsoft might have never have came into existence. And who knows? Maybe to this day, there would not be personal computers in our homes. Maybe there would be no Internet.

Without the Internet and the personal computer, I wouldn't have made my F.U. Money and been able to live such a luxury lifestyle. So thank you, Bill Gates.

WHY I NEVER APOLOGIZE FOR BEING CONFIDENT

I never apologize for being confident. It's because of my confidence that I'm able to write this book so you can benefit from reading it. You get to benefit from my so-called "arrogance."

I would even go so far to say that people who DO NOT reach their true potential are being selfish. They are not giving the world what they could, none of the rest of us can benefit from what they could have contributed.

Maybe it's a cure for a disease. Maybe it's a new technology. Maybe it's a new book. Maybe it's a new song. Maybe it's a new invention. Maybe it's a new idea.

If this is your attitude, not only are you ripping yourself off, you're ripping your family off from the income you could have earned and the lifestyle you could have provided them. You're ripping the world off if you don't go out there, market to people, and let them know what you have to offer.

Think of the people you can help. Think of the lives you can change. Think about your family. You owe it to yourself and also to OTHERS to reach your true potential in this life.

DEVELOP UNSTOPPABLE SELF-CONFIDENCE NOW

Early in my career, I wasn't as decisive and I wasn't as confident. I developed both over time by having successes.

If I had waited around to grow my confidence, I never would have started. So I had to fake it until I made it, trusting that my confidence would grow in the process.

LOKISM #41

You can't be of ANY value to others until you first value yourself.

Money and accomplishment will give you confidence, because in your mind you will now have a track record. You will begin to believe that you can make it happen again and again.

F.U.M.A.

F.U. MONEY ASSIGNMENTS

1. *Most people don't keep a very good record of accomplishments. Take inventory of your past accomplishments, and recognize that they are important and real. Think back to all the things you've succeeded at.*

Past Accomplishment #1 _____

Past Accomplishment #2 _____

Past Accomplishment #3 _____

Past Accomplishment #4 _____

Past Accomplishment #5 _____

Past Accomplishment #6 _____

Past Accomplishment #7 _____

Past Accomplishment #8 _____

Past Accomplishment #9 _____

Past Accomplishment #10 _____

Past Accomplishment #11 _____

Past Accomplishment #12 _____

Past Accomplishment #13 _____

Past Accomplishment #14 _____

Past Accomplishment #15 _____

Past Accomplishment #16 _____

2. *Now leverage your past accomplishments for present-day success. If you ever feel you lack confidence, say to yourself:*

"Damn, I have done _____ before. I can certainly do _____ today. I CAN do this."

CHAPTER 16

YOU CAN MAKE MONEY OR EXCUSES, NOT BOTH

I've met tens of thousands of people in my business career. I've heard all of their excuses about why they can't make their F.U. Money, and I want to list them here for you. Study this list and see how many of these phrases sound a little too familiar.

- If I didn't have a spouse or family who...
- If I had enough "pull"...
- If I had money...
- If I had a better education...
- If I had good health...
- If I only had time...
- If times were better...
- If other people understood me...
- If conditions around me were only different...

- If I could live my life over again...
- If I didn't fear what "they" would say...
- If I had been given a chance...
- If I had a chance...
- If I could do what I really want...
- If I were only younger...
- If I were only older...
- If nothing happened to stop me...
- If other people didn't "have it in" for me...
- If I had been born rich...
- If I could meet the "right" people...
- If I had the talent that some people have...
- If I dared to assert myself...
- If I could speak the language...
- If I only had embraced past opportunities...
- If people didn't get on my nerves...
- If I didn't have to keep house and look after the children...
- If I could save some money...
- If my boss only appreciated me...
- If I only had somebody to help me...
- If I lived in a big city...
- If I were only free...
- If I weren't so fat...
- If I weren't so thin...
- If I weren't so bald...
- If I weren't so ugly...
- If I weren't so pretty...
- If I weren't so handsome...
- If I didn't have big breasts...

- If I didn't have small breasts…
- If I was better in bed…
- If I wasn't SO GOOD in bed…
- If I could just get a break…
- If I hadn't failed…
- If everybody didn't oppose me…
- If I had married the right person…
- If my family weren't so extravagant…
- If luck were not against me…
- If I lived in a different neighborhood…
- If I had a business of my own…
- If my family understood me…
- If I could just get started…
- If I had the personality of some people…
- If my talents were known…
- If I could only get out of debt…
- If I only knew how…
- If I didn't have so many worries…
- If people weren't so dumb… (that's my problem)
- If I were sure of myself… (that's NOT my problem)
- If I hadn't been born under the wrong sign…
- If I hadn't lost my money…
- If I didn't have a past…
- If other people would only listen to me…

As you can see, I've heard it ALL!

THERE'S ALWAYS A GOOD JUSTIFICATION FOR FAILURE

Some of these excuses were my own at one time. I came to North America when I was a kid and I couldn't speak a word of English. So I guess I could have used the excuse, "I can't make it big because I can't speak the language, so what can I do?"

I mean, why even try to make it big in a foreign country when you don't even speak the damn language and the culture is completely different from yours? I had all the rights (or excuses) in the world to be a failure.

Even today I still speak with an accent. Some of my friends still say I sound like Jackie Chan! Sure, I had a lot of excuses in my head why I couldn't be successful: my accent, my looks, my height, lack of communication skills, lack of academic intelligence, lack of contacts. I could go on and on. I had to fight all these personal inner battles. I had to overcome these negative beliefs, just like you.

YOU WON'T MAKE YOUR F.U. MONEY UNTIL YOU GET YOUR HEAD SCREWED ON STRAIGHT

My objective here is not to give you some big psycho-babble motivational talk. However, like it or not, the biggest reason people don't make their F.U. Money is psychology.

LOKISM #42

The amount of money you make is closely related to your self-image.

It's what's going on in your head that's holding you back. I'll prove it.

It's been my experience that I can take two people and give them the same exact step-by-step instructions on how to start a F.U. Money business, with all the tips and strategies. One person will take the information and skyrocket to success. The other will take the same information and fail miserably.

Now why is that? When I first started mentoring other entrepreneurs, I thought it was my information. It turns out that wasn't it at all. It was the difference in the psychological makeup. Bottom line: one person believed she could do it, so she did it. The other person did NOT believe he could make it. So guess what? He didn't make it!

Psychology is a HUGE part of making your F.U. Money, like it or not. That's why I've spent a whole lot of time preparing you for the mindset in this book. If your mindset is right, if your head is screwed on straight, then everything else is a piece of cake.

You can go out there and get the "how-to" all you want—it's readily available. You can meet the people you need to meet. You can develop the skills you need to develop. That's the easy part. But if you don't have the psychology right, you'll fail. Case closed.

AN EXCUSE IS NOTHING MORE THAN A WELL-PLANNED LIE

So today, I've turned all these so-called excuses and disadvantages I had into advantages. For example, I'm five-foot-eight. I'm not tall, but I always tell people that when I feel short I just stand on my wallet (interesting what money does to your self-esteem)!

I used to fear public speaking worse than death, because of my accent. But then I began to look at my accent as something that gave me a distinctive voice. Now I've turned my number one fear into a valuable financial skill.

So what excuses do you have? What made-up stories do you have in your mind that are holding you back from making your F.U. Money? Are they even real?

Remember, you can make excuses or you can make money, but you can't do both! Face your excuses and see them for what they really are: obstacles that you've made up in your mind. When you blow past them, you'll make your F.U. Money that much faster.

ARE YOU ADDICTED TO YOUR STRUGGLES?

Do you know that some people are actually addicted to their struggles?

Now you might be saying, "Dan, I follow what you're saying so far but this just sounds too crazy to be true. This doesn't make any sense!"

Think about it. When someone asks you how things are going, how often do you respond with something negative, like, "Oh man, it's been a tough day. So-and-so problem happened. Wah, wah... cry, cry." Be honest.

Why the hell do you say negative, whiny shit like that? It's like a knee-jerk response for most of us. Most people don't even realize they do it. It's like their brain is trained to spew negativity *automatically.*

I'll tell you why this happens: it's because we get empathy. "Oh, poor you" —BOOM! That second you get attention and approval instantly. It's a hell a lot easier to get empathy than to actually fix the damn problem. I don't care how successful or unsuccessful you are, all of us want attention, approval, love, and affection, including me.

When you were a baby and you cried, what happened? Mommy or daddy ran to you and showered you with love and affection. Do you see how this stuff is ingrained into our brains since childbirth?

Some people spend so much fucking time feeling sorry for themselves, it's sickening. They don't want to take responsibility or actually do anything to change their circumstances. Instead, they "win" by losing. They "win" by not making mistakes, by complaining, by justifying—and they become addicted to their struggles.

Some friends of mine always seem to experience ups and downs. They make a lot of money, they lose it, they make a lot of money again, they lose it again. If they were to instead focus all that energy they have feeling sorry for themselves on changing what's wrong with them, their problems would eventually disappear or, at the very least, become less evident.

Now, of course, this is easier said than done. It is easier for me to type this stuff up for you to read than to do it in real life. Even I constantly have to fight and struggle and not be addicted to this kind of stuff.

Why waste so much time and energy thinking what's wrong with your life? I mean, let's face it: life is hard. Things don't always fall into place like you want them to. All of us get an unwelcome visit from Mr. Murphy from time to time. And even when things work out, something can come along to screw it all up again. Shit happens.

LOKISM #43

**Life ain't fair.
Business ain't fair.
People ain't fair.
Get over it!**

Bottom line: you can continue down the self-pity path for the rest of your life looking for sympathy and alienating all those who have any interest in working with you. You'll die a miserable human being who contributed nothing.

Until you take responsibility, get your head screwed on straight, and understand the psychology, you'll never have F.U. Money. The choice is always yours.

CHAPTER 17

THE POWER OF SETTING D.I.G.

I believe in setting a D.I.G.—Daily Income Goal. Now, a lot of people have income goals. For instance, they want to make one hundred thousand dollars, two hundred and fifty thousand dollars, one million a year or whatever.

What I do is a little different. I have those yearly, monthly, and weekly goals, but it's the daily income goal that I focus on.

Let me give you an example. Let's say your income goal is ten thousand dollars a month, which is a good goal for most people.

Now, what most people do is review their income goal at the end of the month, see how close they came to hitting their target, make some adjustments, and then keep going, right?

A better way is to divide your income goal by thirty days. In this case, your D.I.G. is approximately $334. So the first question when you get up in the morning should be, "What am I doing today to make 350 bucks?"

Then ask yourself, out of all of your big to-do lists and all of the corresponding tasks, which task is most likely to help you reach your D.I.G.? Once you determine this, you will then be focusing only on your daily goal—NOT your monthly income goal.

Ask yourself these questions:

- Are we making more money today?
- What's the most efficient use of my time right now?
- What's the payoff of this activity?
- What objectives do I want to accomplish?
- What must I do to accomplish these objectives?
- In what sequence should I complete them?
- What would Dan do in this situation?
- What would massive action look like?

It's simple. If you're not hitting your D.I.G., then you're not hitting your weekly income goal. If you're not hitting your weekly income goal, then you're definitely not hitting your monthly income goal. Does that make sense?

It's stupid to wait till the end of the month to find out, "Oops, I'm off track." So instead, every day, the daily minimum is your focal point—that's your priority. Everything else is CRAP.

It doesn't matter if you want to make ten thousand dollars a day or $350 a day. Whatever the DAILY number, that's your focus. So always ask yourself FIRST, "What am I doing today to make my minimum for the day?" Every single day, day in and day out.

Now, you might ask, "Dan, what if I miss a day?" Well, the next day you have to do something that will make you twice as much. In this case you have to make seven hundred dollars to make it up.

What if you do better and go over your daily income goal? Say, for instance you do five hundred bucks? Well, Congratulations! Give yourself a pat on the back for doing a good job. But don't slow down or relax… keep going!

You can be very busy and still be very unproductive. Returning phone calls, answering calls, e-mails, paperwork—all that kind of stuff—NONE of those things help you generate money or make sales.

BUSYNESS IS A FORM OF LAZINESS

You must do stuff that will put money in your pocket.

You might say, "But Dan, all I've got is a job and I am working for somebody else. I only get a paycheck once a month. I can't set a D.I.G. There's not a whole lot I can do to increase my daily income."

LOKISM #44

Hitting your daily income goal is your number one priority every day. Everything else is bullshit.

You're right. There ain't much you can do. Your income is fixed. How much you earn is determined by your boss. You're not in control.

You can't do things that will drastically increase your income if all you have is a job. There's no room for creativity and growth. That's exactly why it's almost impossible to make the F.U. Money working for somebody else.

You better start a business on the side that will give you an extra stream of income. In the beginning, your daily income goal can be as simple as one hundred dollars PER DAY. Then when you hit that target, double it, then double it again, and so on.

When I first got started, one hundred dollars was my daily target. I was thrilled to make a hundred bucks a day! Then two hundred. Then four hundred. Then eight hundred. Then sixteen hundred—and so on. Keep counting and upgrading.

Today, my D.I.G. is fifteen thousand dollars.

To Bill Gates and Warren Buffet, that might not be a lot of money. Bill Gates probably wouldn't get out of bed for fifteen grand a day, but for Dan Lok, it's good. It's damn good. It's more than I'll ever need.

Did this happen overnight? No. It took time and tremendous effort to get to this point. Do I always hit my daily target? No. But most of the time I do.

This D.I.G. method has helped me over the years to become extremely productive. So now I have **$15,000** in big numbers on the wall in my office. I get cranky if I don't make that amount of money every day.

Now it's your turn. If you follow my lead, it won't be long before you make boatloads of money each and every day.

CHAPTER 18

WHAT YOU CAN LEARN FROM SOUP NAZI ABOUT DEALING WITH CLIENTS

AND DOING BUSINESS ON YOUR OWN TERMS

If you've ever watched *Seinfeld*, you'll remember the episode of the Soup Nazi. It's the famous episode where Jerry, George, and Elaine go to this new soup stand that Kramer has been raving about. The owner of the joint is referred to as the Soup Nazi because of his attitude and his short temper. Plus, there was a certain "procedure" you had to follow when you ordered the soup.

Jerry explains the procedure for ordering the soup to George, and they go stand in line. When it comes time to order the soup, George wants bread and the Soup Nazi says, "You have to pay for it."

When George gets upset and refuses to pay for it, that's when the Soup Nazi says his world-famous catch phrase "No soup for you!"

What allows him to do that?

There's a very important lesson here for all of us. And that lesson is this: don't take shit from ANYBODY. Have the attitude that nobody is allowed to take you down or insult you without your permission.

So why could the Soup Nazi do that? Because he makes the best damn soup there is! He has no need to please anyone, no need to be popular, or politically correct—nope, because he knows his soup is good. You either want it or you don't want it. You don't like the way he does business? Well, just piss off. You're gone.

And that's the way I've always operated my business. You can always make money. You can always get new clients, new business, and you can always start new businesses. Working with asshole clients is never worth the grief. It's just not worth it.

Doing it this way allows you to focus more on creating a great product and spending your time, efforts, and energies with people who actually like you. They like what you have to say, they like your products—they are raving fans that are willing to spend money with you. This is SO important.

Sometimes when I send a broadcast e-mail to my list with an offer, I'll get some hate e-mails. These are people who are pissed off, saying things like, "You're just a scam artist… you're just trying to sell me stuff." These people are always immediately removed from my list. They're not going to be my customers anyway. Who gives a shit what they think?

This is a business, not some charity drive. Sure, I'm here to help people, but I'm also here to make money. So if anyone on my list is not cool with that, they're history—I take them off the list. The hell with them.

If you don't remove this negative crap, it has the power to take you off your game. It's funny as hell, but sometimes you can get ten, twenty, thirty, fifty really nice e-mails and good comments; people telling you how great your product is and how they have benefited from you and your wisdom, and how much they enjoy your service. But one nasty e-mail from some prick can make you temporarily forget all the good comments and ruin your whole day.

That's why I don't see all of my e-mails. I have my assistants filter them all so I don't see any of the abusive or insulting stuff. I only see the legitimate ones that I would want to know about. Other than that, I'm not interested.

You can conduct business on your own terms.

At this point, I can get rid of anyone in my life that I don't want, don't like, and don't want to deal with. I can fire clients at will—and I have.

I have refunded a twenty-thousand-dollar check to a client and told him to fuck off. I can disqualify any prospects as I feel like it. I fired this client mainly because he was just a pain in the ass.

It wasn't always like this. When I was broke, there was a time when I had

LOKISM #45

Nobody is allowed to insult you without your permission. Nobody is allowed to say anything bad about you without your agreement.

no choice but to take on asshole clients that I shouldn't have because I needed money to put food on the table. More often than not, I've found that the aggravation far exceeds the money in these cases. You may be able to relate to this. I learned this lesson the hard way.

If you have clients you don't want to deal with at the moment, get rid of them! Nobody is ever going to show up at your door, point a gun at your head, and say, "You have to take me on as a client." Nobody's ever gonna do that.

You can choose. You can disqualify them. You can get rid of them.

WHY MOST OF YOUR CUSTOMERS SUCK

Conventional wisdom says, "Treat everybody that comes through your door equally well!" Fuck that. You've heard of the 80/20 rule, haven't you?

It means that 80 percent of your revenue comes from 20 percent of your clients. All customers are not created equal.

Most of the time, the other 80 percent are dud clients. It doesn't make them bad people. It's just that they're not the right clients for you. They might be the perfect clients for somebody else. But for you, they're simply not a good fit. Dump them. Refer them to somebody else. Send them away.

Dud clients cost you more money and energy long-term, but chances are good that you only deal with them because you want their money. When you do that, your integrity has gone out the window.

You're actually doing these clients a disservice by keeping them. You owe it to them and yourself to refer them to someone who can and will do their best work with them.

Why have clients, or anyone for that matter, in your life that frustrate you, bore you to tears, and drain the life out of you?

Clients are replaceable. Money is replaceable. Time is NOT replaceable. The seconds you used up reading this paragraph are gone forever. You can't get them back. Doesn't it just make sense to place a very high value on the most precious commodity you possess—your time?

I am very selective about whom I do business with. I have a zero tolerance policy:

LOKISM #46

You'll become effective only by being selective.

- If I dread the thought of having lunch with you, I am not doing business with you.
- If we have a meeting and you're late, you're not doing business with Dan Lok.
- If you're a negative or toxic person, I don't want you in my life. It's that simple.

Let me give you an example.

A DAY WITH DAN—ONE-ON-ONE COACHING ON MY TERMS

I offer a full-day coaching strategy session, I call it a "Day with Dan" for which successful entrepreneurs fly in to see me from all over the world.

We lock ourselves in a room from nine a.m. to five p.m., and during this time we will find the hidden opportunities and profits within their business.

They can ask as many questions as they want and pick my brain. Basically for that day, I will treat their business like mine, consult with them, and give them ideas on how to make a hell of a lot more money.

By the end of the day, they'll walk away with a step-by-step blueprint on how to take their business to the next level.

Clients prepay me twenty thousand dollars a day for a "Day with Dan." Again, this is business on my own terms: they come to me, I don't go to them. They fly to Vancouver to see me and I'm paid twenty thousand dollars BEFORE I do the work, not after.

LOKISM #47

Poor people get paid AFTER they do the work. Rich people get paid BEFORE they do the work.

Most people who have a job work the entire week, two weeks, or a month and then they get a paycheck.

Heck, even most consultants work this way. They consult, and then they send an invoice. A lot of times they have to chase the client to get their money.

I'm a coach. I'm a mentor. I'm NOT a bill collector. I don't do that crap. I get paid before I do the work. And the funny thing is, I do a "Day with Dan" typically once a month, sometimes twice a month if I feel like it, and I have a three- to six-month waiting list.

YOU CAN'T BUY ME

One time, a very successful Chinese businessman wanted to hire me for a "Day with Dan." You know those Chinese take-out restaurants you see in the food court? You know where they serve spring rolls, fried rice, sweet and sour pork?

Well, he owns fifteen of those restaurants. Anyway, he told me, "I'm busy," so he asked me to fly and see him. "Come on, Dan, I will make it worth your while," he said.

"No," I replied.

He tried again. "Dan, tell you what. I will pay for the flight, first-class, and I will put you in a nice five-star hotel. You can come in for a day and take a look at my businesses. You can leave first thing in the morning the next day."

"No, it's not the way I do business," I repeated.

"How about this? I will pay you twice of what you normally charge, all you have to do is just come and see me."

"You don't understand. You can't buy me. My policy is, you come to me, I don't come to you. You seem like a nice guy and I do want to work with you. But if you're not comfortable with that policy, then I guess we're not doing business."

Finally he said, "Fine, I will come to you."

In fact, he was more impressed that I stood my ground. Since he's a wealthy guy, he can pretty much buy anyone most of the time. And yet I said, "NO. I don't care how much you pay, I'm not coming to you."

Ironically, one of the things he wanted to learn from me was how to do business on his own terms. He turned out to be one of the best clients I've ever worked with.

By the way, if you'd like to book a full day of coaching with me, simply visit **www.fumoney.com** and let my assistant know you want to book your Day with Dan, as well as the details of your project and what you're looking to get out of your day.

If you qualify, she'll get back to you with your choice of available days. Then, once she receives your check, she'll send you an outline of what to expect for the day (which is eight hours long), details about hotels, and a confirmation.

I can conduct business the way I want to conduct business; I can say no to any deals, projects, or people that I don't want to deal with. I am free to work with whomever I want because I don't need anybody's money. And when you don't need money, it comes to you faster, easier, and quicker than you ever thought possible.

It's an interesting oxymoron.

Why does this happen? It's because you're not needy.

When you need money, you are NEEDY. It's a lot like dating....

You know those times when you really like a girl, and you get all hyped up and psyched and emotionally attached? In other words, you become needy. You become too emotionally attached to the outcome.

And then when you approach her and ask her out, you get rejected. Why?

Because needy is creepy. If you were an attractive woman, would you want to date a wussy and needy man? I don't think so.

Instead, when you're just being yourself, you're casual about it and you don't take it too seriously. Then when you ask her out, what happens? BOOM! You score!

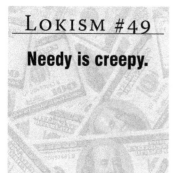

LOKISM #48

When you don't need money, it comes to you faster, easier, and quicker than you ever thought possible.

LOKISM #49

Needy is creepy.

It's the same thing with money: when you don't need it, it comes to you faster and easier.

F.U.M.A.
F.U. MONEY ASSIGNMENTS

1. *If money were no object, how would you run your business?*

2. *What kind of clients would you want to work with?*

3. *What would your new business policies be if you changed them so you get more money and more satisfaction?*

CHAPTER 19

THE SIMPLE SYSTEM THAT HELPS YOU MASTER YOUR TIME
AND TAKE CHARGE OF YOUR LIFE

Your time, knowledge, and energy are your most valuable commodities. If you really think about it, time is all you have. Your time is your life. That's why I absolutely hate it when people waste my time. It's worse than stealing money from me.

I can always make money. But I can never make more time. Customers are replaceable. Money is replaceable. The only thing you can't replace is time. The time you just spent reading this book—it's gone. It can't be replaced or replenished.

So, it just seems so damn obvious to me that your top priority should be protecting the only asset you have that can't be replaced.

Unfortunately, most people give more thought to where they're going to go for lunch than how they're going to protect their time.

Here's the question that you need to ask yourself and answer every single day:

"How do I protect my time and energy so that I am only spending it on those things that will take me closer to my F.U. Money?"

You might ask, "What's this got to do with making money?" Are you kidding me? EVERYTHING! How you use your time ultimately determines how much money you make.

LOKISM #50

How you use your time ultimately determines how much money you make.

Time management doesn't exist. You can't manage time. You can't make it go faster or slower. You can't make time move forward or backward, and you can't make up for lost time.

What you can do is manage yourself and how you choose to use the time that you have. The richest people in the world have the same amount of time as the poorest people in the world. We all get twenty-four hours a day, 168 hours a week and fifty-two weeks a year. No more, no less. So time management is really self-management.

So, the question is not can you better "manage your time," because you can't. The real question is what do you focus on NOW? Do the actions you take on a daily basis move you forward in the direction you want your life to move? Or do your actions move you away from your priorities?

The second thing you have to know is how much your time is worth. I call that your **magic number**.

The reason you're not making the kind of money that you want, and the reason you're not working the amount of hours you want, is because you have not made it a point to continually increase the worth of your time.

Do you understand how important this is? To make the kind of money you really want in your business, you must continually increase the worth of your time.

All time has value; the way you think about time and the way you think about yourself will affect everything that happens to you inside and outside of your business for the rest of your life.

And guess what? If you don't value your time, nobody else will. And why should they, especially if you don't even know how much your time is worth? I'm always shocked at how many people don't have any idea what the value of their time is, or even how to increase the value of their time.

So here are two critical questions for you:

1. Do you know what your time is worth?

2. Do you know what your time needs to be worth to achieve your F.U. Money Targets (F.U.M.T.s)?

> ## LOKISM #51
> **Rich people value time. Poor people value stuff.**

If you don't know what your time is worth now, or what it needs to be worth to achieve your goals, then you can't make effective decisions on what activities you should be spending YOUR time doing and what activities you should have others do FOR you.

So let's take a minute and figure out what the value of your time needs to be to get you where you want to be.

Here's my assignment for you, and it's very simple.

First question: What is the amount of money that you would like to make this year?

Write it down: _____

In this case, let's use a million dollars. Let's say your F.U.M.T. is to make a million dollars a year (if that's too much, then use one hundred thousand dollars. If it's too little, you can use two or ten million dollars, whatever).

Let's say you work eight hours a day, 220 days a year. That's 1760 hours a year. Okay, now take the million dollars and divided that by 1760 hours. It equals approx. $568. But that's NOT your magic number. To get your magic number, you take $568 and multiply it by three to allow for unproductive vs. productive hours. That equals $1,700.

What is your magic number? _____

Why multiply by three? Because I know you don't spend eight hours a day working productively—nobody does. Be honest with yourself: you're not productive all the time. I know I am NOT.

So, to make a million dollars a year, each of your hours has to be worth $1,700. That's your magic number. Why is the magic number important? Because you have to constantly ask yourself the question, "Is what I am doing RIGHT NOW worth $1,700 an hour?

If the answer is NO, it gets you to start thinking seriously about Return-On-Time-Invested (ROTI). In other words, how are you investing your time, and what's your return on that investment? This number helps you to quantify what the hell is going on in your life. Are you investing your hours well?

Let's say you spend an hour mowing your lawn. That just cost you $1,700! Why the hell would you do this if you can get a company to do it for fifty bucks? How are you gonna make a million bucks a year when you spend your time doing twenty-dollar-an-hour work? (And you wonder why you don't make the kind of money you want to make.)

You MUST eliminate the need for you doing the activities that do not match up with the value of your time.

This is why I don't wash my car. I don't go grocery shopping. I don't vacuum my carpet. I don't do bookkeeping. I don't do ANY of this crap that I can pay someone fifteen or twenty bucks to do!

I am only a master of three or four things in my life, and they are things that make me a LOT of money.

I don't even know how to change a light bulb. I'm not kidding. I don't know how to wash dishes. I don't know how to fix my toilets. And I don't WANT to know. I don't give a shit! I wouldn't enjoy doing any of this stuff anyway, even if I did know how to do it.

LOKISM #52

It's better to be really good at one thing than average at a bunch of things.

I know, some people will think, "Aw, come on, Dan, you should clean your car yourself… do your taxes yourself… do (whatever) yourself. Be a man. A little hard work never hurt anybody. Besides, it's good for you. It's an honorable thing to do."

Fuck that! I do what I love doing… what I'm great at doing. There's no "honor" in doing things I'm not good at. What's the point? Do you think you have a greater chance of going to heaven if you spend your life doing things you don't like? I don't.

There's no honor, no joy, no payoff in this life or any other life for doing that which I'm not good at and that which I don't like. People who think I should do this stuff can kiss my ass.

Let me give you another example: I don't know how to cook nor do I have the desire to learn.

If I did cook, I would probably suck at it, so I wouldn't even enjoy eating what I created. Why work so hard to create a shitty meal that I wouldn't even want to eat?

Lokism #53

"Do what you love and the money will follow" is a lie. It should be: "Learn to love the activities that are capable of producing the largest sum of money - then the money will follow!"

Instead, I have a chef named Judy who designs highly nutritious meals just for me. She does all the shopping and brings the utensils needed to prepare the meal to my home. Once a week, she prepares my meals using the highest quality and freshest ingredients available.

When she's done cooking, my dinners are packaged and stored in my refrigerator and freezer. Then she cleans it all up and I don't have to lift a finger.

When she's done, I have a week's worth of healthy, great-tasting dinners waiting for me—it's awesome! All I do is come home to a wonderful smelling house, follow the heating instructions, and in thirty minutes or less I have a delicious home-cooked meal!

Think about this scenario for a second. Chef Judy loves to cook. I hate to cook. She's had years of training, and she's a whiz in the kitchen. She prepares foods for me that are well-balanced and healthy, so I benefit from good nutrition without having to think too hard about it. I pay her to do what she's good at—what she enjoys doing—and because of it I'm free to do what I'M good at doing.

If more people thought this way, we would ALL be better off, wouldn't we?

F.U.M.A.

F.U. MONEY ASSIGNMENTS

Make a list of activities you do on a daily basis. Evaluate each task you do. Can you delegate this task?

Task to be delegated	Who should accept the delegation?	How many hours do you free up?	Value of those hours?	Date you'll delegate the task	Delegated task complete (check off)

CHAPTER 20

THE AMAZINGLY SIMPLE TECHNIQUE THAT BOOSTS YOUR DAILY PRODUCTIVITY

I don't work on Friday, Saturday, or Sunday, so basically I have a long weekend almost every weekend. Most of the time I work three or four days a week, unless I have an important project going on, when I may choose to work Friday as well.

I work as little or as much as I want. Because I don't work seven days a week, I have to make sure that when I do work I am super-productive. I have structured the way I work in a very productive manner—such as not taking unscheduled incoming calls.

A lot of people have the tendency to pick up the phone when it rings. It's like we've been trained like monkeys. Not me. I set my own time schedule and make others work around me. I ONLY do prescheduled phone appointments.

And isn't it true that 90 percent of the time the incoming calls aren't that important anyway? Isn't it true 90 percent of the time they aren't THAT urgent?

In fact, here's what my voice mail says:

"You've reached the office of Dan The Man. I am either on the phone or away from the office. Please leave your name, your phone number, and the purpose of your call. Please don't expect me to call you back right away. I'll get back to you whenever I am available. Thank you for calling."

So you might think, "Well, aren't you difficult to work with?" I wouldn't use the word *difficult*. I'm just different.

LOKISM #54

You can sell people on doing business with you on your terms, as long as they know what's in it for them.

Besides, it's more productive for both parties anyway. How? Because you know when you schedule a call with me, I'm not doing anything else. I'm expecting your call. It eliminates phone tag. You know you have my undivided attention during that period of time.

Bill Gates schedules his appointments in six-minute increments. I have mine in fifteen-minute increments. I set aside blocks of time for everything that I do during the day, including checking e-mails, which I usually do after lunchtime. And once I do, I don't check my e-mails anymore and I work on something else.

ARE YOU WASTING TOO MUCH TIME ON E-MAIL?

I know some people check their e-mails ten times a day, especially if they have an Internet business.

A lot of Internet entrepreneurs "screen-suck" all day. Whenever they have some extra time, they go to their computer and check their e-mail. Once they're done, they'll surf around the Internet a bit. Then they'll check the auctions they're bidding on eBay. And then they'll log on to MySpace, Facebook, or whatever.

Once they're done, they'll start all over again, back to e-mail! Are you one of them? Be honest with me here. How the hell do you get anything done if you're constantly interrupted and distracted?

I used to get about four hundred e-mails a day, but now with my virtual assistant checking my e-mails, I maybe only get twenty or twenty-five. So I block out around half an hour to go through my e-mails, reply to them, log off, and forget about it.

I check my orders in the morning and once again in the afternoon, because I want to know how much money I'm making. I don't use MSN and instant messenger. I don't want to be interrupted whenever someone has a "brain fart." Instant and quick access doesn't equal productivity.

FEELING STRESSED AND FAILING TO MAKE PROGRESS TO YOUR F.U. MONEY?

As an entrepreneur, don't you sometimes feel overwhelmed and confused? You get up in the morning and you have this whole pile of shit you have to do. You don't know what to do first.

Everybody talks about prioritizing, but how exactly are you supposed to do it?

To me, there are only two kinds of activities in a business: profit producing activities and non-profit producing activities.

Non-profit producing activities include talking to your friends, surfing the Internet, checking e-mails, answering your phone, checking Web status, organizing your office, and bookkeeping, etc.—activities that don't put cash in your pocket.

LOKISM #55

Your number one job each and every day is to do everything you can to drive more revenue and profit into your business.

Profit producing activities include creating new products, marketing your products, improving your marketing process, managing moneymaking projects, raising capital, finding new ways to acquire customers, setting up joint venture deals, setting up strategic partnerships, creating systems, and hiring good people to run your businesses,—activities that put cash in your pocket.

Out of all the tasks you have to do, don't spend a lot of time doing the ones that don't make you money. Delegate and outsource them! They're NOT the most important tasks.

THE NUMBER ONE COMMON TRAIT OF ALL F.U. MONEY MILLIONAIRES

People fail because of broken focus. Most business owners who struggle are busy with the day-to-day responsibilities of the business and only take action on what's getting their attention at the moment. They don't think or act strategically. Big mistake.

Why do people get distracted so easily? Because they don't know what they want—they get sidetracked.

When you're very clear about what you want—when you're focused—it's like taking the sunlight that's beaming down to the earth and having a microscope in your hand. You have the ability to redirect the sun's energy into something that's intensely hot. By focusing the energy, you've essentially created a laser beam, which can easily create a raging fire. That's the kind of focus you need to make your F.U. Money.

> ## LOKISM #56
>
> **Distraction is the only true luxury of poor people. Laser-beam focus is mandatory for success.**

So what does being focused mean on a day-to-day basis? It means knowing your strengths, what you're good at, and possibly getting rid of other things altogether.

People come to me all the time and say things like, "Dan, I run a small business. I'm doing some day trading. I'm doing some real estate. I'm thinking of starting another business. How come I'm still not making any real money?" And my answer is usually, "Because you're involved in too many businesses, that's why!"

Sound familiar? If that sounds like where you are now, try to pick the business that has the highest probability of making your F.U. Money. Get rid of the others and see what happens. You'll be shocked by the result.

F.U.M.A.
F.U. MONEY ASSIGNMENTS

Make a list of activities you do on a daily basis: business-related, work-related, and personal. List even the small tasks such as mowing the lawn or photocopying.

1.	16.
2.	17.
3.	18.
4.	19.
5.	20.
6.	21.
7.	22.
8.	23.
9.	24.
10.	25.
11.	26.
12.	27.
13.	28.
14.	29.
15.	30.

Identify the five activities from the list above that generate the most income for you or your company. These are the activities on which you want to focus the most time and energy.

1. _____
2. _____
3. _____
4. _____
5. _____

.

part 4:
THE F.U. MONEY BUSINESS

CHAPTER 21

THE NUMBER ONE REASON WHY PEOPLE DON'T MAKE THEIR F.U. MONEY

One the biggest reasons people never make their F.U. Money is that they get sucked into the latest moneymaking schemes, such as the latest real estate trend, the latest pyramid schemes, the so-called "opportunity of a lifetime."

When I was broke, I was all over the map. I was the guy who bought all those home biz and opportunity magazines and responded to all the how-to-make-money-from-home ads. I got into day trading, mail order, vending machines—you name it.

I was always looking for the next big thing, the next big idea. Anything that would make a quick buck. Bottom line: I wanted to get rich quick without doing the work. I never made the kind of money I am making now when I was jumping from one thing to another. Not even close.

It's like people who try to lose weight by buying all these gadgets, pills, programs, and potions that are supposed help them lose weight. The REAL formula is simple: it's proper diet and exercise. Get off your lazy ass and exercise, and don't shovel all that fatty food down your throat.

LOKISM #57

Most people don't want the truth. They're just looking for things that sound good.

It doesn't get any simpler—but people don't want *simple*. They want to buy the magic pills and machines that will do the work for them instead. They are just opportunity seekers, jumping from one idea to another.

In fact, I know an entrepreneur who runs a very successful Internet company offering weight loss solutions. The funny thing is that he sells about fifteen different programs, all from different manufacturers. He knows that once he finds a person who will buy one weight loss pill, he or she will try just about everything else. This person will try one thing for a few months and then switch to something else.

WHO REALLY MAKES MONEY WITH FRANCHISES?

Franchising has made a lot of people a lot of money, but mostly the people who sell them. Franchises have made a lot of other people either poor or the equivalent of slaves after they buy one.

In any transaction you're either a consumer or a promoter. When you're buying a franchise, you're a consumer. It's the person who SOLD you the franchise who made the money—because they were the promoter. And in the end, they win.

I'm not saying never buy a franchise, I'm just saying to be aware of where you stand in the deal. If you ever want to make your F.U. Money, you have to be a promoter. You want to be the one that's collecting the cash, not the one that's giving it out.

ARE YOU BEING SCAMMED?

So what are some of the typical things that suck people into scams? Let me share with you a few things I've heard through the years. When you hear words like these from now on in the business world, HOLD ON TO YOUR WALLET:

- "I'm a good Christian." (Truth is, good Christians don't need to tell you that's what they are. You'll already know by their actions).
- "If I may be perfectly honest…" (That means that the guy hasn't been honest from the beginning.)
- "It's the opportunity of a lifetime."
- "This can't fail."
- "You've got to get in now."
- "Don't miss the boat."
- "May God be my witness." (Look out for lightening bolts on this one.)
- "Don't worry, your money is fine."
- "I'll take care of everything; don't worry."
- "The situation is temporary."
- "This is the best thing you'll ever do."
- "This will exceed your expectations."
- "It's just a standard document, just sign here."

Why do people fall for these things? It goes back to lack of education, lack of self-esteem, and greed. If you let these character flaws rule your business decisions, there are people in the business world who will FEED on you—people will fuck you over.

I should know—I've been fucked over many times in my business career. So it's okay to be cynical. Be aware. Ask questions. And watch your wallet.

CHAPTER 22

THE MONEY SECRET SHARED BY BILL GATES, RICHARD BRANSON, AND WARREN BUFFET

Whenever you catch yourself looking to find some source outside yourself to create wealth with ease overnight—watch out.

Now, you might ask, "Dan, doesn't this contradict with what you just said in F.U. Money Myth #6 about getting rich quick?'

No. Don't take what I said out of context. I'm not saying you can't get rich quick—you definitely CAN. I'm saying not to look for someone ELSE to make YOU rich quick. Nobody can make you rich—only YOU can make yourself rich.

So when you hear the message, "We do all the work, you don't have to lift a finger, and voila, you'll make a gazillion dollars!" BEWARE. It's just like those illegal pyramid schemes that have been going on forever—where ONE person talks you into it by telling you that "if you get in soon enough and sign enough other people up quickly, you'll make a fortune. It's a groundbreaking opportunity." Hold onto your wallet and RUN!

Gambling is a good example. Gamblers gamble because they hope to win a lot of money without doing any work. If you're the casino owner—very smart. If you're the gambler—not so smart.

I sincerely hope you will stop being an opportunity seeker or just a wannabe who only DREAMS of F.U. Money but doesn't want to put in the effort to get there.

LOKISM #58

All wealth schemes have the fatal flaw of taking YOU out of the equation.

To make your F.U. Money, you MUST be part of the equation. You can't make money without work, without risk. No luck is involved. No "hot new thing" is required. What IS required is work. Smart work.

Look at the most successful people on the planet: Bill Gates, Richard Branson, Warren Buffet, and Oprah Winfrey. There was never a hot moneymaking scheme involved up front. It was always the vision to create a business, deliver a lot of value to a lot of people, and solve a problem. That's what made them rich.

So who would you rather learn from? Oprah—or some slick-talking, get-rich-quick schemer? Think about it.

OPPORTUNITY SEEKER VS. F.U. MONEY MILLIONAIRE

What's the difference between an opportunity seeker and a F.U. Money millionaire?

Opportunity Seeker:

An opportunity seeker sees an opportunity arise and grabs it. These people are always looking to make lots of money from the hot opportunity of the moment. Their only criteria is, "Can I make quick money doing this?"

For instance, today it's nothing down real estate. Tomorrow it's mail order. The next day it's day trading, and yesterday it was some other hot concept that's already forgotten.

Opportunity seekers buy lots of products and courses about how to get rich quick, yet they use only a few of them. And the ones they do use get abandoned when the next so-called "easy" way to make money comes by. Their only question is, "What is the easiest way for me to make money right now?"

Opportunity seekers have no strategy, hopping from one approach to another. And while they may have some income goals, they have no vision of the business they would need to create in order to achieve them.

And since they don't have a clear vision, they can't follow a detailed plan to accomplish it. So they end up with the hope that this is going to be it—that this is finally their chance to make it big. They are especially prone to fall victim to the business-in-a-box products that promise huge rewards with little or no effort.

F.U. Money Millionaire:

The F.U. Money millionaire, on the other hand, is a different animal together. These people have a clear vision of what they want their business to become. The biggest opportunity is always inside THEIR business, not the hot product everyone is talking about this week.

The F.U. Money millionaire has an end in mind, a vision. These people know what the business is going to look like when it's done. They develop different alternatives for its accomplishment and choose the approach they think is most probable.

The F.U. Money millionaire understands what his strengths and weaknesses are—so he builds a business based on his strengths.

LOKISM #59

Definition of a F.U. Money millionaire: a person with a vision who orchestrates other peoples' time, talents, and money to make his or her vision a reality.

The F.U. Money millionaire also understands that a business is a financial vehicle to get from point A to point B. She isn't emotionally attached to any ONE particular business.

These people are mostly concerned about how the business would serve them. They continually ask, "Does this move me closer to my F.U. Money? Is it what I really want to do?" They build their business around their lifestyle preferences and always ask the question, "How is my business going to serve me?"

Opportunity seeker vs. F.U. Money millionaire.

The choice is yours.

CHAPTER 23

THE NINE CHARACTERISTICS OF AN IDEAL BUSINESS

The U.S. government sends one of their agents to a Native American tribe to convince them to go to school and get jobs so their society will be better off.

The agent figures out that he has to go "top down" and talk to the chief to get him on the program. If he can get the chief on board, then everyone else will follow.

"Chief, we'll get you into a great college or trade school," he says. "We'll pay for it, pick you up in the morning, drop you off, pick you up after school, and drop you back here. We'll get you a tutor, make sure you get good grades, graduate, and get a good education."

The chief asks, "Why would I want to do that?"

"Well, because then we can get you a good job and you can work for a good company."

The chief asks, "Why would I want that?"

"Well, because then we can drive you to work, pick you up if necessary, give you a nice suit to wear... you can start working at a good job and make a salary."

The chief asks, "But why would I want that?"

"Because if you get a good job and work for a good solid company for forty years, you get to retire."

The chief asks again, "But why would I want that?"

"Well, because then, when you retire, you can do whatever you want for the rest of your life. You can sleep if you want to, you can hunt, you can fish...."

The chief says, "But I am DOING THAT RIGHT NOW."

It's one thing to make money—and it's another thing to make money and operate on your own terms. They are two different things.

LOKISM #60

It's not just HOW MUCH money you make, it's HOW you make the money.

If you ever intend to make your F.U. Money, you first must put yourself in a position to do so. If you're gonna spend your time doing something that has absolutely ZERO chance of making you F.U. Money, what is the only outcome? You're not gonna make it.

Unfortunately, that's exactly what most people do when they get into business for themselves. Look at the kind of businesses they get into: they buy expensive franchises, they open a restaurant, they become a manufacturer, they open a retail store.

They invest a lot of money, time, and effort, taking unnecessary risks and piling on grief so they can go make a little bit of money, swapping hours for dollars. Why? Because they think that's the way they're supposed to do it. They were not taught any different.

Since they're in control, they think that's the path to F.U. Money, when all they've really done is swapped one job for another, one crazy boss for another. It's stupid.

You have to START with the right vehicle. You see, there are only three reasons to be in any business (in order of priority):

1. CASH NOW: You want to make money now, not in three years... not five years from now... not hopefully when you "cash out" at some undetermined time "in the future." NOW!

2. CASH MONTHLY: It's critical to have cash flow coming in on a consistent basis to pay your bills and live comfortably.

3. CASH IN THE FUTURE: If you can "cash out" and sell your business for a ton of money sometime in the future, that's fantastic.

These are the only three reasons to have a business, unlike what others want you to believe: the government believes that the purpose of a business is to pay taxes, the unions believe that the purpose of a business is to provide jobs to the community, and *some* entrepreneurs believe that the purpose of a business is to provide jobs for themselves.

Bullshit.

The purpose of a business is NOT to provide jobs or support your employees. If you do, that's nice, but it's a side benefit. The purpose of a business is so that you can make your F.U. Money. Very simple. If you help people make a living along the way, wonderful. But that's not the purpose. The purpose of the business is to support YOU—to make you RICH. That's the only purpose.

F.U.M.A.
F.U. MONEY ASSIGNMENTS

1. *What's the most you can make at what you currently do?*

2. *How much do you need to invest to get started?*

3. *Could it be that your business is just another job where you happen to be the boss?*

4. *Does your business provide more income than you need to live comfortably and buy the things you want?*

5. *Is what you're currently doing worth all the time you're putting into it?*

6. *Does it have a prayer of making you F.U. Money?*

7. *If you can't work, will your income keep coming in? (very, very important)*

It's critical that you take a few minutes and answer these questions. Once you have, next determine WHAT your business will be.

BUILD YOUR BUSINESS AROUND YOUR LIFESTYLE PREFERENCES

"The true value of a human being is determined
primarily by the measure and the sense in which
he has attained liberation from the self."
-ALBERT EINSTEIN

After several business failures at an early age, I made a decision that I would no longer do anything just to make money (which is how a LOT of people operate).

I made a decision to look at my "vision" and determine what I REALLY WANTED. I got down to the fundamental questions: "What do I really want out of my life? What do I want my business to look like? What do I want my life to look like two, three, five, ten years from now?

I did something a little different. I locked myself in a room, took out a pen and a notepad, and wrote down exactly what I wanted for my life. I wrote out every detail of what I wanted for my business—how I wanted my business to serve me, besides just providing me with money.

- It wasn't "how can I make a quick buck doing this?"
- It wasn't "what do other people want from me?"
- It wasn't an idea that someone else had sold me as "what I really want."

It IS what does Dan Lok <u>REALLY</u> wants.

I decided that I was going to figure out exactly what my perfect lifestyle looks like, and build my business around my lifestyle preferences.

So that way, I wouldn't get sucked into the latest moneymaking schemes, stuff that would get me sidetracked. Because I would now have clarity. What follows are the nine characteristics you should look for when choosing your next business opportunity.

Characteristic #1 – Do What You Love

What are you interested in? What are you passionate about? What subject or topic do you have a lot of knowledge about? What are people always coming to you for advice about?

You should pick a business where you at least have some interest, versus something you have absolutely no interest in.

If you do something just for the sake of making money, that's okay, but it's shortsighted. Sure, you'll make some money, but honestly, life is too short. There are so many things to do to make money, so much opportunity in the world, why not do something that you love?

I love what I do and I am damn good at what I do. Any aspect of my work that I don't love and that I'm not good at is done by others. By doing it this way, I've set up my business in such a way that I never get bored.

That's one of the reasons I keep working even though I've made enough money now that I could stop working altogether. Every day I get up, I can't wait to work. A lot of people who live boring lives are downright jealous of me because they wish they had something this exciting in their lives.

There's a saying you've probably heard of: "I love this so much that I would do it for free." I think that's MORONIC. Here's what I want you to say instead: "I love this so much that it's the ONLY thing I would do for money."

Characteristic #2 – Stable, Growing, Long-Term Demand

Who told you that they want what you have to offer? What makes you think people would pay for it?

The foundation of your business must include:

a) evidence that the market wants to pay for what you're offering

b) evidence that they want to pay for that solution from YOU

c) strong evidence of the brilliance of your solution

Contrary to conventional wisdom (again!), competition is good: it means there's money in the marketplace.

Many people come to me and say, "I've got this idea. Nobody has ever done it before." That's probably because nobody has made a fucking dime doing it! I'm not saying you can't make a fortune with new ideas; others have made good money doing so. But remember—pioneers mostly just end up with arrows in their backs.

That's why I prefer just to sell something people already buy. I don't want to have to convince them they need my product. They already know they need it. The question is just whom they're going to buy from. Then my job is only to convince them that I deliver more value than the competitors and therefore it would be in their best interest to buy from me.

Characteristic #3 – Be Portable

Imagine working from a beach, or from your holiday home in Brazil. With technology today, that dream can easily become a reality.

A portable business means you can operate your business from anywhere—home, office, beach, or anywhere you want to live or visit. You can be in business anywhere and have access to the Internet anytime you want. You may prefer the beach or being poolside. Heck, one of my students even works off his boat on the lake.

I personally like to work from the comfort of my own home. I hate to get stuck in traffic. It drives me nuts. I can't stand it. When I get up in the morning, it's a two-second commute to my office. I grab a cup of green tea (I don't drink coffee), and I just start working. I can be in my pajamas, underwear, shorts and a T-shirt, whatever. In fact, I'm home so much that my neighbor thinks I'm a drug dealer!

Can you imagine how much time you would free up if you didn't have to commute to work?

Characteristic #4 – High Profit Margin

There are a million ways to make a million dollars. One of them is to sell low profit margin items to tons of people—the mindset known as "feed the masses and you'll dine with the classes."

Well, I say the hell with the masses—or even more, the hell with low profit margins! There are some businesses that have five, 10, and 20 percent profit margins, and people still get into these businesses.

But you know what the problem is with low profit margins? There's no margin for error. That's suicidal. There will ALWAYS be errors. If you set yourself up in a low margin business, you're asking for trouble. It's a one-way ticket to bankruptcy court.

A friend of mine bought a dollar store so he could be his own boss. It's always been his dream to own a retail business. The profit margin of a typical dollar store is 10 percent. That means when he sells something for a buck, he gets to keep ten cents. Later the same friend told me, "Dan, the two happiest moments of my life were the day I bought the dollar store and the day I SOLD it."

Succeeding in business is difficult enough. Why make it even harder on yourself by starting a low-profit margin business?

I like BIG profit margins—the bigger the better. For me to even consider a business, the profit margin has to be at least 100 percent and up. So if I am selling something for two hundred dollars, I want to keep AT LEAST one hundred dollars for myself. Preferably it's 200 percent, 500 percent or even more, otherwise I won't get into that business.

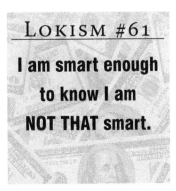

LOKISM #61

I am smart enough to know I am NOT THAT smart.

Characteristic #5 – Scalability

A business must have the potential to grow fast by adding additional streams of income. I must be able to sell additional products and services to existing customers, as opposed to being a one-time sale business. I simply will not get into a business if there isn't a potential for big, back-end profits.

And ideally, you can scale a business using systems, technology, and outside vendors versus just hiring more employees. This way, not only is it easier to grow fast, but you can scale back down if sales revenue drops for a period. Otherwise, you'll be like those corporations that, when sales are slow, have to fire a bunch of people to scale down.

Characteristic #6 – Low Start-Up Cost

You must be able to start a business with a few thousand dollars, not millions of dollars. If a business requires millions to get started, it means you have to go out and raise capital. NOT that raising capital is bad, but to do so, you have to give away ownership and equity. Plus it takes you much longer to recoup your investments.

On the other hand, if you only spend ten thousand dollars starting a business, you only have to make ten thousand dollars in profits to get all your money back. After that, it's all gravy. Once your business grows to a certain point, you can bring in outside investors if you want. By that time it's easier to raise capital and you don't have to give away as much equity because you now have a proven business model.

Characteristic #7 – Requires Little or NO Staff

Have you heard the saying, "You're only as strong as your weakest link?" I'm here to tell you that's a BIG FAT lie. Here's the truth: "If you spend your entire life working on your weaknesses, at the end of your life, you'll have a lot of strong weaknesses!"

> **LOKISM #62**
>
> **If you spend your entire life working on your weaknesses, at the end of your life, you'll have a lot of strong weaknesses.**

If you want to make your F.U. Money as quickly as possible, you have to focus on your strengths and outsource everything else. I know my strengths (which are few), and I know my weaknesses (which are MANY).

One of my weaknesses is management of employees. I couldn't manage my way out of a paper bag. I'm NOT a micromanager, but I am a macro-thinker—a concept guy.

So I want few employees, preferably ZERO. Right now, I run a multimillion-dollar company that is completely virtual. I have two virtual assistants and a lot of independent contractors all around the world working with me (not for me). I have a powerful team—all without the hassle, headache, and expenses of full-time employees. I hire them on a project-to-project basis, so I don't have anyone on my payroll.

I run over fifty websites, yet none require my daily presence. Some require a little of my time, and others require absolutely none.

People ask me all the time how I can get so much done. But what they don't know is, I DON'T—my team does. All I do is videoconference with my virtual team occasionally to brainstorm and create plans for growth, and exchange e-mails with them regularly.

My job is simply to put the right person in the right place, give them the resources and direction they need to get the job done right, and help them maintain focus.

Characteristic #8 – Low Overhead

I prefer to keep money in my pocket versus paying everybody else and not myself. Even to this day, I keep my business lean and mean.

I could easily get a fancy office or hire some drop-dead gorgeous assistant, but I don't. Why? Because I prefer cash in one place: my pocket.

Conventional wisdom says that you want to invest your profits back into your business. You know what? That's a load of CRAP.

Lots of people take the profit from their business and sink it all back into the business—that's just dumb.

Ask yourself this: if you can't hold onto the money and invest it personally, what value will it be to your business when the business gets in a down cycle or is not doing well?

There are always ups and downs in business. If you don't think your business has a down cycle, you haven't been in business long enough.

So think… if you put all your money and earnings back into your business and don't take any money out, and then a downturn happens and your business goes broke, where do you go for help? Think about it. You're broke, too, since you didn't keep any of the money!

LOKISM #63

Suck your business dry like a vampire. Take money out all the way.

Rather than reinvesting all your profit back into your business, my motto is to suck your business dry like a vampire. Take money out all the way.

Now don't take me out of context here. I am not saying you have to take all your money out so you have no operating capital or cash flow. What I AM saying is that you take out as much cash as possible and leave just enough money in the business to keep it running.

Also, as the owner of a business you want to PAY YOURSELF FIRST, not your employees. I know some employers who pay their employees first before they pay themselves—bad idea.

If I'm NOT happy then nobody is happy, so I want to make sure I get paid before everybody else. As a business owner, you need personal cash flow. You need to put cash in your pocket to feel like you're succeeding.

Now, you might be thinking, "Oh, Dan, I can't take money out. My business won't survive." If your business can't survive just because you take some money out, you either need to fix it or you need to walk away from the business.

If you're in a business that would normally be very profitable, yet it's being mismanaged (by YOU), then you suck—you've gotta fix yourself. Perhaps you've compared your current business with the characteristics I've listed in this chapter and come to the conclusion that you're in the wrong business to begin with. If that's the case, good!

Now you've realized that you're in a business that sucks, so you can stop wasting your time.

Life is too short. What's the point of keeping a business that can't even provide you more income than you need to live comfortably and buy the things you want?

Characteristic #9 – Money Coming in While You Sleep

How can you ever have freedom if you're working in a business that requires you to be there every day? That's not freedom, is it?

Bottom line: if your income is determined by the number of hours you work, you'll NEVER make your F.U. Money, and you'll never have true freedom. You simply must have money that comes in while you sleep.

> ## LOKISM #64
> **If your business can't make it without money, then your business probably can't make it with money.**

What's crazy is that dentists and doctors study for eight, ten, twelve years in medical school and get heavily in debt just so they can swap hours for dollars the rest of their lives. In essence, they fix teeth and write prescriptions all day to pay off their school debts.

I love my doctors and am grateful that I have them around when I need them. But to me, that's not a very exciting way to spend your life. (If you're a dentist or doctor reading this book, you know exactly what I am talking about!)

If I were to ask a dentist or a doctor, "Let's say you've already made your F.U. Money, and you never have to work another day in your life. Would you still keep you doing what you're doing?" Most of them would reply with no hesitation, "Nope. I would get the hell out of here."

Getting in debt and studying for years so you can swap hours for dollars makes no fucking sense.

LOKISM #65

Life and time are the same thing. If you're wasting your time, you're wasting your LIFE.

I want a business that has the potential to make me a lot of money with minimum involvement from me.

I have two hobbies; one is ballroom dancing. I do cha-cha, rumba, and Latin dance, where I compete at an amateur level (not professionally).

I also practice martial arts. I especially enjoy martial arts because it enhances my self-discipline and improves my physical health at the same time.

"It's nice to know that you can kick the ass of anyone at the table. What more do you need to know? That image of yourself extends to all areas of your professional and personal life. Physical well-being says you're disciplined, you are a winner."

-DONNY DEUTSCH
HOST OF THE BIG IDEA

I couldn't agree with Donny more. That's why I'm a bit of a health nut myself. I don't drink, smoke, or do drugs. I'm big on exercising and working out, because that's how I stay healthy so I can enjoy life to the fullest. Besides, what good is it to be rich if you're so sick and tired that you can't enjoy the money?

I like this old Spanish proverb: "Health, wealth, and the time to enjoy it."

That's my motto.

So these are the nine characteristics of an ideal business. Now, compare these defining features to your existing business. How many elements does your business have? How can you incorporate these elements into your current business? If you were to start all over again, would you buy your own business from you?

If your answer is no, then the time to get out is NOW. You need to have a heart-to-heart with yourself and take inventory of what you really want in life, and how you propose to get it.

The only vehicle that I found that meets all these criteria is an Internet business. The Internet has brought me fortune and fame. I would not have made my F.U. Money so fast without the Internet. So if you haven't started a business yet, you should seriously consider starting an Internet-based business NOW. Do it in your spare time if you have to. Once your Internet business is generating twice as much income as your current job, you can quit your current job if you want to.

Or, if you have a business, but it's not currently Internet-based, you have two choices. One: transition that business from offline to online as much as possible. Use the Internet to streamline your operation, attract new customers, or outsource difficult and tedious tasks, etc. Or, two: get out of the business you're in and start an Internet business. It's that simple.

This may sound harsh, but again let me remind you—if you ever intend to make your F.U. Money, you must first put yourself in a position to do so.

CHAPTER 24

HOW ORDINARY PEOPLE MAKE EXTRAORDINARY INCOME ONLINE

Last Sunday morning, I got up, had a little breakfast, and drank some green tea before firing off an e-mail that took me about fifteen minutes to write.

Then, I closed up shop and went shopping with my girlfriend for some new ties and new shoes.

Sunday is, after all, a day when people should rest. I even went to a black tie party later that night. All in all, it was a fantastic day I must say!

On Monday, when I got back to the office, I checked to see how many orders my e-mail had generated. How about a WHOPPING

$25,618.70! All from one e-mail… a simple message I wrote in fifteen minutes flat. Not bad for fifteen minutes of work, huh?

I'm not telling you this to impress you but to IMPRESS upon you that you can also create incredible success online, with the help of the right knowledge and tools.

Besides, if I don't toot my own horn, no one but me will ever know about my success—and as a result, I'll have zero credibility. First rule of business: toot that damn horn and tell the world how amazing you are!

LOKISM #66

If you don't toot your own horn, no one will toot it for you.

I know some people will take this as nothing but braggadocio and arrogance. Frankly, those people are losers. Winners will sit up and pay attention while the losers get busy pointing fingers, judging me, whatever. Honestly, I couldn't give a shit what the losers think.

I'm assuming that if you've made it this far in this book, you're sure as hell not a loser. I therefore am also going to make the assumption that YOU, TOO, would like to learn how to make money on the Internet while you sleep. Right? Good. Because that's exactly what I'm going to show you how to do in next few chapters.

HOW MUCH MONEY CAN YOU MAKE?

Making five figures a month online is really no big deal. Making six figures a month is one hell of a feeling. And seven figures a month, well, that's my goal for this year.

Maybe you're thinking, "Dan, you can say things like making five figures a month online is no big deal because you're THE MAN, but do REAL people make that kind of money?" Here's the thing—it's NOT just true for me. I've helped thousands and thousands of "ordinary" people make a fortune on the Internet. It's not a matter of luck or "being at the right place at the right time" or any of that nonsense.

One of the most recent successes is Charlie Cook, a marketing consultant to Fortune 500 companies that include AETNA, AT&T, Cendant, GTE, and Pitney Bowes, as well as midsized companies like Citizens Utilities and Hartford Steam Boiler, publications that include Fortune, Hemispheres and Forbes and numerous small businesses: **www.MarketingForSuccess.com**.

Charlie's passion lies in helping small business owners and marketing professionals discover a better way to attract clients and grow their businesses. Charlie found me on the Internet and enrolled in my mentoring program. When I started working with him, he was already very successful, but he wanted stop trading time for money as a consultant.

Together we turned his experience and knowledge into a line of educational products. Now people can buy his materials and do things for themselves. As a result, Charlie's now raking in half a million dollars per year online.

Another one of my protégés is a photographer named Shane Goldberg. Shane tried to use Photoshop to edit his photos, but he struggled to learn the program. He thought to himself, "If I have this problem, I wonder if other photographers have the same problem?"

He then launched **www.ProPhotoSecrets.com**—a membership site devoted to teaching people all the Photoshop tricks and tips.

He's since retired from the photography business and now makes a nice five-figure income every month working from home. This allows him to spend quality time with his seven-year-old daughter. He's now on track to build a multimillion-dollar Internet company. I am very proud of him.

Another one of my success stories: Darren LaCroix, the owner of **www.Humor411.com**. He is the guy to call when other professional speakers want to learn how to make their audiences say WOW!

In 2001, Darren outspoke twenty-five thousand contestants from fourteen countries and became the World Champion of Public Speaking. He now sells an enormous amount of products and services on the Internet and his website is raking in hundreds of thousands of dollars a year.

LOKISM #67

Every problem is a product.

I have another protégés. Take Rob Palmer, a former struggling freelance writer. Rob started a website called **www.GoFreelance.com** from his basement and turned it into a multimillion dollar company. His site is now one of the leading freelance sites on the Internet.

I can fill this ENTIRE book with rags-to-riches stories like these from my students.

Which leads to me to wonder… how anyone can be lukewarm about the Internet? How can anyone be skeptical or unconvinced that it is not only legitimate but that it's a damn smart way to make money while you sleep?

People who are still skeptical of the Internet fall into one of these three camps:

1. People who are too lazy to get off their ass and learn how the Internet works.

2. People who are afraid of change. These are the ones who don't want to stretch their comfort zones—people who are stuck in the rat race. They play not to lose instead of playing to win.

3. People who believe other people can do it, but not them. They say, "I'm not a techie. I'm not a computer person. I'm too old for this." "I can't" rarely means that you actually can't. What it really means is "I don't want to/I don't know how/I'm too damn lazy."

GROW AND PROMOTE YOUR OFFLINE BUSINESS ONLINE

Nowadays, if your business doesn't have a website, you have zero credibility. It's almost mandatory, regardless of what business you're in.

By having even a simple informative website about you and your product or service, you open an instant, FREE door to potential clients that you never had before.

I can't think of a single business that can't benefit from being on the Internet and I don't care what business you're in.

If you have an existing business, you can use the Internet to:

- Directly sell your products and services directly
- Educate and "pre-sell" your customers
- Follow up with your existing customers
- Provide quality information for your potential prospects so you build trust with them
- Generate leads for your offline business

If your business is doing well offline, you can dramatically increase your sales and profits by building your presence on the Internet.

And if you don't have a business yet, the best place for you to start is on the World Wide Web. It's by far the cheapest advertising tool that you can have, plus you get to have global exposure.

More and more people research and make their purchases online. If they're looking for a new car, a new house, a new book, you name it—guess where they go?

LOKISM #64

There is no easier, faster, and more certain way to create massive wealth in record time than the Internet.

To the search engines. And when you learn how to harness the Internet to give people what they are ALREADY searching for, you can make a fortune.

The Internet is not going away. If anything, it's going to grow bigger, better, and much more lucrative. So get on the Internet and get on NOW.

CHAPTER 25

HOW I WENT FROM RAGS TO RICHES ON THE INTERNET

To give you the nitty-gritty of what it takes to succeed online, it's important to tell you my story. So let me share with you how I got started: how I made money, how I lost money, and how I've made my F.U. Money on the Internet.

I figured out much of what I know now from the school of hard knocks.

In March of 1997, I was confused as hell. Like most people, I had no life direction. I wasn't sure what I wanted. By that point, I'd experienced many business failures and I was up to my eyeballs in debt. My self-esteem was low. Let me tell you—it was NO fun waking up in the middle of the night worrying about how I was going to pay the bills.

I had read *Think and Grown Rich* by Napoleon Hill. Although I had done a lot of thinking, there wasn't enough riching. Then I read *How to Win Friends and Influence People* by Dale Carnegie. I just didn't know how I could "influence" my friends to loan me money to pay my bills.

I did all the things that most people do, like buying self-help books and tapes, going to seminars, and even walking on hot coals. I did all the things that the gurus teach: goal setting, positive thinking, affirmation, visualization—all that stuff. Most of it didn't work for me. I was still broke. I wasn't making enough money. I certainly wasn't fulfilling my dream.

That's when I made a discovery that changed my entire life's direction. I stumbled across a book in a used bookstore called *Scientific Advertising* by Claude Hopkins.

The title appealed to me because all my business failures up until that point had boiled down to one problem: lack of customers. I bought the book for three dollars. I must have read it ten times in a row. That book changed my life.

By the way, *Scientific Advertising* now falls into public domain, so if you want a FREE copy, you can download it at my website: **www.fumoney.com/freegifts**.

The book revealed to me that there's actually a science to marketing and attracting clients. From that point on, I was hooked on this marketing stuff. I started buying all the marketing books I could get my hands on. I started studying ads and sales letters. I wanted to know what makes people tick and what motivates people to buy.

Most people buy magazines to read the articles. I would buy magazines to read the ads. People throw away their junk mail; I read my junk mail before I opened my bills. In fact, I was getting all kinds of junk mail because I purposely ordered stuff from mail order companies so I could see different offers and pitches. I wanted to be sold to.

HOW I ACCIDENTALLY MET MY MENTOR

I noticed that a guy by the name of Alan Jacques kept sending these sales letters, inviting me to various financial seminars. His sales letters really stood out.

They were powerful and compelling, and always filled with fascinating stories. Alan Jacques knew how to craft a killer sales letter. He was a marketing genius. I kept all his letters in three-ring binders and found myself signing up for all the financial seminars he offered.

When I was attending one of these seminars, I noticed a gentleman sitting next to me. I didn't pay too much attention. But when I saw that his name tag said "Alan Jacques" I was speechless.

I thought to myself, "Could this be THE Alan Jacques? It couldn't be. No way."

Finally, I couldn't help myself and I asked him nervously, "Are you Alan Jacques?"

"Yes, I am."

"Oh, my goodness. I'm on your mailing list. I've been getting your letters. That's why I'm here."

"Good. I'm glad you like the seminars." Alan thought I was referring to the seminar.

"No, you don't understand. I mean I love your sales letters! I love the way you sell and market. I actually keep all your sales letters and put them in three-ring binders to study them."

"REALLY?" He looked surprised and flattered at the same time. "You know, most people just throw them in the trash can."

"That's because they don't know the value of these letters. They don't understand it isn't the thing—it's the thing that SELLS the thing."

"You're right, young man. You know, you're pretty bright for your age." There was a smile on his face.

LOKISM #69

One conversation can change your life forever.

That's when I stepped out of my comfort zone and asked one of the smartest questions I've ever asked: "I don't mean to impose, but can I buy you lunch?"

"Hmm… what the heck? I gotta eat," he agreed.

THE MILLION-DOLLAR YEAR OF MY LIFE

At lunch, we just clicked. Alan took me under his wing and I became his apprentice. For a full year, I worked like a slave for peanuts. But I didn't care. I wasn't working for him to make money. I worked for him because I wanted to learn.

That's when I found out you could put words on a piece of paper, put it in an envelope, mail it out, and people would send you money. It was a revolutionary discovery for me. I was amazed. I said to myself, "This is the best way to make money in the world without a gun." And depending on how you look at it, it's corrupted me forever more.

LOKISM #70

If you could get there on your own, you would already be there.

Here I was, a copywriter for his company. I would do all the grunt work, write the letters and then take the bags of envelopes to the post office and mail them. That was the million-dollar year of my life. I got a million dollars in education in that year.

Finding a mentor to show me the ropes was the answer for me. It may not be the answer for everybody, but it certainly was for me. Literally, my life was changing in a few months because I had learned to turn words into cash.

MAKING A SIX-FIGURE INCOME AS A COPYWRITER

By October 2000, I was making a six-figure income as a professional copywriter. Not bad for a guy who was broke a couple years before, huh? I wrote copy for a lot of best-selling authors, speakers, and various small businesses.

I learned a ton about marketing and business because I got a first-hand look inside many successful (and not so successful) businesses. When you're writing sales copy for clients, it naturally leads to consulting. They'll often ask you, "How should I mail these letters? Who do I mail them to? How do I follow up?"

Giving them a sales letter without a strategy is like giving them a computer without telling them how to use it. But I felt like an imposter. Although I was a damn good copywriter, I was no master of business success. In fact, unbeknownst to my clients, I was a master of business failures.

So I got obsessed and started studying as much as I could about business, sales, leadership, management, and finance. In addition, I had the privilege of learning from my clients and my mentors. Eventually I got a grip on what I was doing, and I began consulting with different entrepreneurs successfully.

Here I was running a successful consulting and copywriting business. New clients were finding me—and old clients were hiring me repeatedly. I raised my fees substantially, but it still didn't seem to "scare people away."

LOKISM #71

Never, ever get paid based on hours worked.

As a copywriter, my sales letters had generated tens of millions of dollars in revenue for my clients. I made them rich and happy. (People seem to develop warm feelings for you when you make lots of money for them!)

Business just kept coming and money was rolling in. Things were good. Well, sort of…

But by 2003, I hit a plateau. I had no idea how I could increase my income without working harder. I realized I was simply a high-paid slave swapping hours for dollars. At first, it was fun, even thrilling, but it didn't take long for me to feel trapped inside this so-called successful business. I wanted out.

One day I was approached by a webmaster, who told me, "Dan, you should get a website."

"I don't know," I replied. "I'm getting enough clients just from word of mouth. What do I need a website for?"

"Maybe you can sell a product on the Internet or something."

I wondered, "Hmm… what would I sell?" Then I got an idea.

What if I put some of the most important lessons I had learned up to that point about marketing and psychology into book form? What if I sold that on the Internet?

I pounded out a book called *Forbidden Psychological Tactics*. It contained twenty-seven psychological tactics that marketers and companies use to motivate and persuade people to open their wallets and buy.

I made one hundred copies at five dollars a pop and started selling them for $19.95 plus shipping and handling on the Internet. I was basically making fifteen dollars per copy.

At the time, I had no idea how to set up a website or anything like that, so I paid the web guy five hundred bucks to set it up for me. On the site I had my phone number so people could call me and place an order, or they could send checks to my address. I couldn't accept credit cards or anything like that.

Looking back, I can't believe how stupid I was, making it so damn difficult for customers to buy from me. If you have a website, people want to buy and they want to buy now. If you want to maximize your sales, you have to take credit cards. Here I was making people jump through hoops.

HOW I MADE MY FIRST SALE ON THE INTERNET

Anyway, about twenty days later, I got a check in the mail from someone from California ordering my book! I couldn't believe it. I picked up the phone and called the guy. He said, "Yeah, I saw your web page. I thought your book looks interesting. Send me a copy."

"Wow, this is amazing," I thought. So I started going onto different forums and talking about my book. And BOOM, I got more checks and more calls from people wanting to order my book.

Orders were coming in from all over the world. The second order was from Dallas, Texas, the third from Toronto, Ontario, there was even one from Australia. They sent me checks and money orders, yet I had never talked to them or met with them face to face. I just deposited the checks and shipped the books to them. No fuss, no muss.

Within three months, I had sold one hundred copies of *Forbidden Psychological Tactics*. My entire inventory was gone, and I had made $1,500 in profits.

Now you might say, "Dan, it's $1,500 bucks. What's the big fucking deal?" You don't understand; I knew that if I could make $1,500 doing it part

> ## LOKISM #72
> **Make your first sale online before worrying about getting rich.**

time, if I devoted more energy to it, I could double that or MORE. This could be huge.

CRACKING THE CODE TO EBOOK RICHES

Then I stumbled across the late Corey Rudl's website. He offered a course called "The Insider Secrets to Marketing Your Business on the Internet." THAT spoke to me. I coughed up the money for this massive course—hundreds of pages of content.

There was one particular chapter in the course in which Corey talked about selling digital products on the Internet. It was basically about creating books in digital format and making them available for download, so you didn't have to ship anything—you kept more of the money.

Damn, why didn't I think of that?

There was ONE problem. In order for me to do that, I knew I must accept credit cards on my website. So I applied for a merchant account—and got turned down because they couldn't understand what I was selling. The banks had no idea what an eBook was.

I applied for another merchant account and got turned down again. I was starting to get a little discouraged. Finally, after eight rejections, I got a merchant account. Now I could accept payments on the Internet. Yee-ha.

I immediately called up my web guy and had him turn my book into an eBook (an eBook is an electronic book you can read digitally on your computer or laptop screen). Not only that, but I bumped the price to $29.95 and now I would have no shipping costs. All I would have is the credit card fee. Therefore, I kept 95 percent of the profits!

As my excitement for this Internet business grew, my desire to work with copywriting clients one-on-one decreased substantially. I would rather focus on minding my own business.

I knew I need to develop more products, so I got busy creating and marketing numerous new ideas. Many of them flopped. Some projects were breaking even, but a handful of them were HUGE winners. That's the great thing about business: one BIG win can make up for a lot of losses.

LOKISM #73

The ideas you think will work best often fail. The dumb and crazy ideas you threw out there just for the hell of it often produce the biggest results.

I continued to try different things, make mistakes, and learn from other people. My sales went from $1,500 a month to $2,500 to six thousand dollars and then to ten thousand dollars a month. Then, it kind of got stuck at ten thousand a month.

And then someone told me I needed to build a list. So I started an e-newsletter called "Dan's Rant." When I started building my list, I only had a dozen subscribers. And that included my girlfriend, my friends, and my cousins, but it grew and grew. In fact, today, I have over fifty thousand "Dan's Rant" subscribers.

THE DAY I BURNED THE SHIPS— THERE WAS NO TURNING BACK

And then one day, I just decided I would no longer write copy for anyone else. I fired all my copywriting clients in ONE day. Talk about brass balls.

I called them and told them, "I'm sorry. You're a great client. We've had a great business relationship, but I can no longer write for you. I'm going to pursue my new business ventures. Thank you."

There was no turning back. I had burned the ship and put myself into a financial crisis. Looking back, that turned out to be one of the riskiest, yet one of the best decisions I've made.

That same year, I made a huge investment into a software program that I planned to market to network marketers. The programmer basically ripped me off and overcharged me. Even after I had paid him tens of thousands of dollars, he hadn't done a damn thing. When I found out, it was too late. He took my money and disappeared.

That same year, I started five websites and they ALL failed. I lost almost all of the money I had made from my initial Internet boom. I found out quickly that motivation is good, but desperation is even better. I really had to dig deep to see what I was made of.

LOKISM #74

Failure is a resource. It helps you find the edge of your capacities.

I started really analyzing what worked and what didn't. Why didn't certain things work? What new skills did I need to develop in order to make this Internet business successful?

I started developing a set of principles and philosophies to making money on the Internet. These are fundamentals, not the latest gimmicks or tricks.

Fundamentals are everything, while fads come and go. In martial art, I've learned that an amateur is someone who knows a thousand moves but practices each move one time. A master is someone who knows only a few moves but practices each move thousands of times.

The same concept applies to business. If you aren't getting the results you want, if you backtrack you will see that the cause is that you aren't using the fundamentals to online business success. I'll share these fundamentals with you in just a minute. They are surprisingly simple, but profound.

Then I launched a piece of software called Instant Cash Copy, which helps business owners crank out killer ad copy without hiring an expensive copywriter. It became an instant best-seller and it's still one of my best-selling products.

In the meantime, I started developing more high-end educational products, such as home study programs, manuals, and CDs. With the combination of good traffic-generation tactics, good products, and killer copy, my business took off in a hurry.

I was now back on my feet. My sales in the month of March 2005 reached twenty thousand dollars. I had doubled my previous record of ten thousand. I thought I was something special. I really thought that was a LOT of money.

A few months later, I coordinated with a group of joint venture partners and did a product launch that generated over $101,694.00 in twenty-nine days. I took a lot of that money and started other Internet businesses in various niches.

I began to outsource a lot of the tasks and started building a powerful team. Armed with my experience and skills, I was able to dominate niche markets and multiply my income very quickly.

In 2005, I ended the year doing $467.096.92 in sales. By 2006, I became a millionaire. I doubled that figure in 2007. I doubled that figure AGAIN in 2008. I won't even tell you how much I make this year because you probably won't believe me (not that I care what you think...).

Did it happen overnight? No. Was it easy? No. Was it worth it? Absolutely!

In fact, would you believe that my most successful student is doing better than me? He's making twenty million dollars a year online. That's how powerful the Internet is.

CHAPTER 26

THE 7 GOLDEN KEYS TO INTERNET RICHES

In order to create Internet wealth, you must follow certain disciplines. You must think in a certain way and you must continue to repeat a set of profit-producing guidelines—over and over and over again.

GOLDEN KEY #1 – THE MARKET COMES FIRST

The market you sell to is more important than the products or services you sell. The number one reason people fail is because they spend so much time creating the perfect product without even knowing if there's a market for what they offer. Big mistake.

The absolute key to your Internet success anytime you decide to begin ANY moneymaking project online is effective market research. Remember, people don't buy from you because they understand what you sell—they buy from you because they feel understood.

Too many times I have been guilty of making that mistake. In the beginning of my marketing career, I had a whole lot more losing business ideas than winners. However, as I've refined my market research techniques over the years, my rate of success has improved exponentially. As a result, I've enjoyed a drastically improved income as well.

Research your market and find out what people want and are willing to buy. Not what you think they might buy, not what you think they should buy, but what they're actually spending money on already.

Ask yourself:

- Is the market already buying something similar to what I'm thinking of selling?
- Is this a market where people buy, or is this a market of people who have no money and are looking for something free?
- Is the market big enough?
- Are there existing partners in the market I can joint venture with?
- Am I able to reach these buyers?
- Am I going to be able to drive traffic to my website and get them to buy my products?

Start with a topic that has a future to it. A lot of Internet entrepreneurs fail because they choose a niche without a lot of back-end potential. They choose a niche that doesn't have legs to stand on its own and won't support additional selling opportunities beyond the first sale.

Start with a market that has a viable future to it. Identify niches where people have money and are used to spending it on products within that niche—for example, golfers.

People who are into golf are fanatical about improving their game, and they're willing to plop down a good chunk of change to buy the latest gadgets, read the latest books, watch the latest videos, you name it, just to shave one stroke off their score.

Sell something that is already proven to sell. If you want to find out where money is being made, look no further than where money is being spent.

GOLDEN KEY #2 – CREATE A SIMPLE, EASY-TO-NAVIGATE WEBSITE THAT SELLS

Do you know what the single biggest mistake is that most websites make? They are NOT designed to sell. If you want to strike it rich online, it's crucial that everything on your website is geared to do one thing and one thing only: to sell.

LOKISM #75

Your intimate understanding of your market and core business is the number one ingredient to become rich.

Here's where people always go wrong. If your website doesn't sell—if it fails to convert visitors into customers—then it doesn't matter if you have the greatest products in the world.

It doesn't matter how professional your website looks, or how high your rankings are in the search engines. It doesn't matter how much traffic you drive to your website—none of this stuff means SHIT if your website doesn't sell. Period.

Maybe you want to sell flowers online, or eBooks, or your company's image, or have a membership site, anything else you can think of. The bottom line is the same: you're selling. Your website is not a brochure. You should think of your website as a twenty-four/seven virtual salesperson.

Your website must sell, and it must do so with laser-sharp precision. Once a visitor hits your site, you have only ONE SHOT at making the sale. That's it. There's no second chance.

Every part of your website, from the sales copy to the buttons to the navigation structure, should be built to get your virtual cash register ringing again and again.

GOLDEN KEY #3 – BUILD A BUSINESS, NOT A MONEYMAKER

I learned this one the hard way. I was always after the quick money deals. So I started a bunch of mini-sites, which were supposed to be "push a button and make a bunch of money."

I made good money, but not F.U. Money. I was building a moneymaker instead of a business. Don't make the same mistake I did. That's just not how you build long-term wealth.

A business has assets: customer lists, products, and a brand. Those are your assets. Poor people focus on making money. Rich people focus on building and creating assets that make you money. Little distinction, BIG difference.

GOLDEN KEY #4 – CREATE MULTIPLE INCOME STREAMS IN ONE BUSINESS, DON'T CREATE MANY DIVERSIFIED BUSINESSES

Building multiple streams of income has been popularized by various financial gurus. It's a very powerful concept. It's basically saying, "Don't have all your eggs in one basket." If one source of income dries up, you can always fall back on another income stream of income. You stand a good chance of building wealth this way.

A lot of people misunderstand the concept. For entrepreneurs, trying to make money with ten different businesses is a disaster. It's total confusion. What you really want is multiple streams of income within ONE business—FOCUSED floods of income coming from ONE place.

This way you stand the best chance of succeeding. You'll never reach staggering success by having a million little things going on. Sell to one market and serve the needs of ONE group of targeted people.

Look, I understand that opportunity is everywhere on the Internet. Believe me, I know. I have the "entrepreneurial ADD" as well. I am never short of great ideas.

But trust me on this one: instead of jumping from one market to another, chasing down every idea you ever come up with (and driving yourself crazy in the process), I suggest you squeeze as much money as you can out of one market.

Exhaust every avenue there is for making money within your current market, and you're virtually certain to make more money than you ever would by jumping from one market to the next. Offer multiple products for your customers to buy. Find multiple sources of traffic to drive to your website.

The longer you are in a market, the more you begin to understand the buyers in that market… and the more money you'll make. Create as many ways of making money as you possibly can from your one initial market.

Sure, I have multiple businesses in multiple markets, because I have systems in place. I have other partners in those niches and I have created a model that I can replicate. But I started with ONE market. I suggest you do the same.

Make one thing as big as you can before you move onto something else. Give it your all and you'll make five to ten times more money.

GOLDEN KEY #5 – LEVERAGE THE TIME AND RESOURCES OF OTHERS

You only have so many hours in a day. Even if you don't sleep, there's still just twenty-four hours. You will never be able to work twenty-five hours in a single day. So how do you make more money in your business (regardless of what stage it is currently) if your time is limited?

You must leverage the time of others. Outsourcing has made me a multimillionaire; I wouldn't be where I am today if I hadn't harnessed the power of delegating work to others.

Don't get me wrong. I do work. But to me, my work isn't work. I love what I do. I love my products, my customers, and growing my businesses. And whatever I don't like, I outsource and delegate to others. It becomes their job, not mine.

At the same time, I take a lot of time to play. I only work four days a week. And when I do work, I don't work nearly as hard as people who make peanuts compared to me. Compared to the construction worker across the street, I am a lazy bum.

Working with a shovel is backbreaking work. Even if you were to compare me with the average doctor, lawyer, or accountant who works harder, they would still win.

In case anybody wonders, I am not a techie. I don't know any programming. I don't know HTML. I don't know java script. Frankly, my time is much more valuable than that. I'm not the least bit interested in doing that nerd code stuff. I can easily go to elance.com or guru.com and find someone to do this stuff for me.

If you want to maximize your profits, you must start outsourcing. One of the greatest feelings you'll ever have in your life, as it pertains to your business, is when you have finally learned to pay other people to do those things in your business that you don't enjoy doing so that you can free up your time to do only those things you really want to do.

When you do, eventually you'll get to a point where your business is like mine. There's very little that I do in regards to the day-to-day operation of my business.

LOKISM #76

Let other people and "things" make money for you.

GOLDEN KEY #6 – USE YOUR PERSONALITY TO SELL

People do business with people they know, like, and trust. All of your communication with your customers should be personal and friendly. Write the way you talk. Communicate one-on-one, not one-to-many.

People trust and believe other people far more than they trust corporations. Corporations are big, uncaring, and unbending. On the other hand, people are typically friendly and caring.

Stand out—don't blend in. Be interesting, high-energy, exciting, and entertaining, not boring or bland. Always be genuine and authentic. Figure out who you really are—your core principles and your personality, and then use that in everything you do.

Don't be afraid to tell your story. Share your successes and failures. Reveal your flaws. Why? Facts tell, stories SELL. Can you create an emotional story to wrap around your product or service? Think to yourself, where were you before? Where are you now? Why do you do what you do?

Guess who?

- I was alone.
- I was broke.
- I was overweight.
- I was living in one bedroom apartment.
- I've read more than seven hundred books in the area of personal development and success.
- One day, I decided that my life would change, and never again would I settle for anything less than what I ultimately desire and envision for my life.
- I started applying all that I've been learning from books, tapes, and seminars, and within one year I turned my whole life around.
- I became a millionaire in less than one year. I live in a mansion.
- I've put what I've learned in a bunch of tapes and now I want to you show YOU how to change your life for the better.

Whose story is it? Tony Robbins.

Guess who?

- I had two dads.
- One dad was highly educated and intelligent. He had a Ph.D.
- My other dad never finished the eighth grade.
- Both men were successful in their careers, working hard all their lives. Both earned substantial incomes.
- Yet one dad struggled financially all his life while the other dad would become one of the richest men in Hawaii.

- At the age of nine I decided to listen to, and learn from, my rich dad about money. In doing so, I chose not to listen to my poor dad—my real dad—even though he was the one with all the college degrees.
- I achieved financial independence at the age of forty-seven. And I want to teach YOU the same secrets my rich dad taught me.

Whose story is it? Robert Kiyosaki.

What do these men have in common? They have built their entire business empires around a story. **Personality-Driven Marketing** means developing a PERSONA. Be who you are but AMPLIFY it.

GOLDEN KEY #7 – POSITION YOUR BUSINESS FOR AUTOMATIC GROWTH

As you grow your business, you must position your business in as many ways as possible to automatically make money for you.

There is inexpensive technology available to you for running your businesses that's very powerful. Harness this technology and use it to your advantage.

For example, you can deliver valuable content over time with sequential auto-responder messages sent to your customer's or prospect's e-mail inbox. Another example is building your mailing list twenty-four/seven with a prominent opt-in box and a compelling offer.

If you already have a business online that's making you money, determine exactly what steps you took to get to that money. Identify the core activities responsible for making you money, then use technology or people to repeat those processes again and again.

This piece of advice has made me a lot of money: do more of what works instead of trying to fix what's broken.

LOKISM #77

Stop throwing good money into profit draining projects.

Keep doing the things that have brought you the most money, but focus on fine-tuning the system so you can duplicate and multiply the results. Automate your business as much as possible.

I was on the phone the other day with my uncle, and we were just chatting about family as usual. And he said, "Dan, you're still doing that Internet SHIT?"

"Yes."

"When are you going to get a job like everybody else?"

"Hmmm... never?"

He just doesn't get it and he'll never get it. And that's okay. Most of your friends and family won't understand what you do and how you make your money anyway. Just shut up and make the money... well, and buy them something nice.

The Internet can provide a business that will truly give you the lifestyle, the money, the time, the freedom, and everything else you want.

I really don't think I could find a business that's better than an Internet business. It's the perfect F.U. Money business. If you're committed to making money online, you can and WILL do so. It's never too late to start.

"SO WHAT THE HELL
DO I DO NOW?"

If you've read this far, you've had a damn good dose of Dan.

A lot of people, when they read a book like this, get all jazzed, psyched up, and motivated, but then they asked themselves, "Where should I start? Exactly what is the next step?"

With F.U. Money, I set out to write a different kind of business/success book—one that addresses lifestyle choices as well as money issues. I've read so many books that give you good ideas, but they come up short by not telling you exactly what to do next.

You get excited about the ideas, but life ultimately remains the same. You don't get the results you want. In fact, you would have been better off not reading the damn books at all, because they simply left you confused.

So when I started out, I said to myself, "I'm not going to do that." If I was going to write a book, I was going to do it my way—the Dan Lok way.

In the introduction, I told you that you wouldn't find ALL the answers in this book. I said you would find some of them, but not all. I wrote this book to give you tools and strategies to find the freedom and the answers you're searching for. I wanted my words to compel you to think differently—to find a different and better way to live your life.

And as you can see, I've tried to deliver my message in the most frank and no-holds-barred way possible by talking about my successes, my failures, and my flaws, as well as some of the mistakes I've made and the lessons I've learned. I've tried to do it in plain language, not in some academic mush. I hope you've enjoyed the result.

During our journey together, I know sometimes I can be in your face. That's the kind of mentor that I am. But at least by now you understand what F.U. Money really means; it's more than just a book, it's a new way of doing business. It is a new way of thinking; it is a new way of living.

Now it's up to you to take action. It's up to you to apply these strategies and techniques into your life. These ideas are only as good as YOU make them. They won't do a bit of good unless you take action.

I know some of you will read this book, put it down, and not do a damn thing with it in your own life. You may even tell some of your friends about it, but you won't take the necessary action to change. It will become just another book to cross off your reading list.

I don't want this to happen to you. Change is difficult, I know. The biggest thing that stops us from making the F.U. Money is that we think we can do it alone without any help. We think we don't need to be accountable to anyone.

That's a BIG mistake.

ARE YOU READY TO TAKE CONTROL OF YOUR FINANCIAL FUTURE?

You might say, "I'm committed to make my F.U. Money." But are you really committed? If so, realize this: commitment with no formal structure is really NO commitment at all.

Here's what I mean. Let's say you wanted to lose weight. You might say to yourself and those around you, "I'm committed to losing weight." But the fact is, if you don't schedule your exercise time, maintain a proper diet, and/or get a personal trainer—in other words, have some sort of formal structure in place—than I know you're not really committed to losing weight.

LOKISM #78

Real commitment is commitment with a formal structure.

That's why I've developed a variety of specific programs and resources to help you make your F.U. Money faster and easier—while having more fun than you can imagine.

To gain access, all you have to do is log onto my website at:

www.fumoney.com

I have created an online community—an extensive website to be your F.U. Money resource center. You can go there and join an entire community dedicated to the F.U. Money philosophy.

And now, one more thing before I go…

YOUR COUNTDOWN HAS BEGUN

Now you have NO reason not to get off your butt and DO something. Get moving. You see, there is now a "countdown" running that you weren't aware of. Now that you've completed this final chapter, the clock has started ticking.

Here's the thing: if you don't take some sort of small action towards the F.U. Money within twenty-four hours, I believe it's almost guaranteed that you will never take ANY action towards your F.U. Money.

With every passing second that you don't take action, this book comes closer and closer to becoming yet another book on your shelf, doomed to collect dust amongst all those other volumes you've wasted money on.

And that's a shame. In a way, it would be even worse than if you'd never read this book at all. Now that you've read this book, you can no longer say to yourself, "I don't know how."

I have given you the HOW. If you don't take action now, you have no one to blame but yourself.

So look at your watch. Your twenty-four-hour countdown has begun.

How to Claim Your FREE Bonuses Now

For a complete list of all the free bonus gifts
mentioned throughout this book, please log on to
www.fumoney.com/freegifts.

TreeNeutral®

Advantage Media Group is proud to be a part of the Tree Neutral™ program. Tree Neutral offsets the number of trees consumed in the production and printing of this book by taking proactive steps such as planting trees in direct proportion to the number of trees used to print books. To learn more about Tree Neutral, please visit **www.treeneutral.com**. To learn more about Advantage Media Group's commitment to being a responsible steward of the environment, please visit **www.advantagefamily.com/green**

CPSIA information can be obtained
at www.ICGtesting.com
Printed in the USA
LVHW04s0108230818
587870LV00014B/222/P